Love
Poems

This edition published in 2020 by Arcturus Publishing Limited
26/27 Bickels Yard, 151–153 Bermondsey Street,
London SE1 3HA

AD006339UK

Printed in the UK

Contents

Introduction

Why write about love? Perhaps to capture its joys, or to admit its disappointments – or to say what cannot be said.

In the middle of the 11th century, the Catholic Church was all-powerful across Europe and its embrace was stifling. Then, from Southern France, came the troubadour, singing of the power of love, specifically the power of a lady to ennoble a knight with her love. This was a direct rebuke to the Church's narrow – and patriarchal – strictures.

Kings and queens were quick to welcome these poet-singers to their courts. With royal protection came inspiration: new verse forms developed, and in a world of arranged marriages these were songs to celebrate love. The Church recognized the threat. Here was heresy, and the Inquisition was determined to stamp it out. The troubadours fled, many to Sicily, where they found a culture shaped by Greek, Latin and Arabic influences, which they made their own. Thus, the *sonet* (a little poem) became the *sonetto*, which travelled to Italy, and from Italy to England.

At the court of Henry VIII, Sir Thomas Wyatt and Henry Howard, Earl of Surrey – both included in this collection – were some of the first to experiment with the form.

The sonnet gave voice to hope and to despair. But did the poet hope to love or to advance at court? For the politically ambitious, it seems, love offered a good disguise.

At the court of Elizabeth I, the game continued, though the poems of Sir Walter Raleigh are more straightforward. 'The Nymph's Reply to the Shepherd' is his response to 'The Passionate Shepherd to His Wife' by Christopher Marlowe. Both poems are included here. Raleigh, more than a decade older, is more cynical: he knows that love may fade.

As Elizabeth's reign drew to its close, the sonnet fell from favour, which may well have allowed William Shakespeare the room to innovate. His sonnets express many aspects of love, capturing its obsessions and uncertainties with words that speak for us even today. To that extent, it matters little whether they reflect Shakespeare's own experiences or just his imagination.

William Wordsworth wrote of 'Lucy' as an unrequited love, but it is not clear that she was ever real to him. His friend Samuel Taylor Coleridge suspected not, and yet 'She dwelt among the untrodden ways' captured readers' imaginations almost as soon as it was published in 1800. Its final verse remains one of the most haunting expressions of despair in English poetry.

A real love, painfully unrequited, certainly inspired others. For W.B. Yeats, Maude Gonne was the woman he could never forget. He proposed, she refused, and the next day he wrote 'The White Birds'. Or consider the American poet Sara Teasdale, who attracted many suitors. One, also a poet, loved her but considered himself too poor to propose. She went on to marry a rich businessman. And then to divorce. And, finally, to commit suicide. It's difficult to put these facts aside when reading the four poems that appear in this collection.

For Lord Byron, the facts of his life were central to his poetry, both for good and ill. Lady Frances Wedderburn Webster was the painful inspiration for 'When We Two Parted'; theirs had been a secret affair, so he carried his grief alone when she betrayed him with the Duke of Wellington. Anne Beatrix Wilmot, by contrast, was dressed in black on the evening she attended a ball – and Byron was dazzled. 'She walks in beauty, like the night/Of cloudless climes and starry skies,' he wrote the next morning.

Elizabeth Barrett was also inspired by life. 'How do I love thee? Let me count the ways' is perhaps the most famous of the 44 sonnets that make up *Sonnets from the Portuguese*. She wrote them when she met the man she would later defy her father to marry: Robert Browning, who insisted they were the best sequence of sonnets since Shakespeare's. The acclaim on their publication was immediate.

So too was the praise for Walt Whitman, and the censure. First published in the middle of the 19th century, his collection *Leaves of Grass* included poems such as 'A Glimpse' that describes 'a youth who loves me and whom I love'.

Love, it seems, sometimes has the power to shock.

Just as the troubadours knew.

Loving in Truth

Loving in truth, and fain in verse my love to show,
That She, dear She, might take some pleasure of my
  pain,
Pleasure might cause her read, reading might make her
  know,
Knowledge might pity win, and pity grace obtain,
I sought fit words to paint the blackest face of woe,
Studying inventions fine, her wits to entertain,
Oft turning others' leaves, to see if thence would flow
Some fresh and fruitful showers upon my sunburnt
  brain.
But words came halting forth, wanting Invention's stay;
Invention, Nature's child, fled step-dame Study's blows;
And others' feet still seemed but strangers in my way.
Thus, great with child to speak, and helpless in my
  throes,
Biting my truant pen, beating myself for spite:
'Fool!' said my Muse to me, 'Look in thy heart, and
  write!'

Sir Philip Sidney

How Do I Love Thee?

How do I love thee? Let me count the ways.
I love thee to the depth and breadth and height
My soul can reach, when feeling out of sight
For the ends of Being and ideal Grace.
I love thee to the level of everyday's
Most quiet need, by sun and candlelight.
I love thee freely, as men strive for Right;
I love thee purely, as they turn from Praise.
I love thee with the passion put to use
In my old griefs, and with my childhood's faith.
I love thee with a love I seemed to lose
With my lost saints,—I love thee with the breath,
Smiles, tears, of all my life!—and, if God choose,
I shall but love thee better after death.

Elizabeth Barrett Browning

The Garden of Love

I went to the Garden of Love,
And saw what I never had seen;
A Chapel was built in the midst,
Where I used to play on the green.

And the gates of this Chapel were shut,
And 'Thou shalt not' writ over the door;
So I turned to the Garden of Love,
That so many sweet flowers bore.

And I saw it was filled with graves,
And tombstones where flowers should be;
And priests in black gowns were walking their rounds,
And binding with briars my joys and desires.

William Blake

A Red, Red Rose

O my Luve's like a red, red rose,
  That's newly sprung in June:
O my Luve's like the melodie,
  That's sweetly played in tune.

As fair art thou, my bonnie lass,
  So deep in luve am I;
And I will luve thee still, my dear,
  Till a' the seas gang dry.

Till a' the seas gang dry, my dear,
  And the rocks melt wi' the sun;
I will luve thee still, my dear,
  While the sands o' life shall run.

And fare-thee-weel, my only Luve!
  And fare-thee-weel, a while!
And I will come again, my Luve,
  Tho' 'twere ten thousand mile!

Robert Burns

To His Mistress Going to Bed

Come madam, come, all rest my powers defy;
Until I labour, I in labour lie.
The foe ofttimes, having the foe in sight,
Is tired with standing, though he never fight.
Off with that girdle, like heaven's zone glittering,
But a far fairer world encompassing.
Unpin that spangled breast-plate, which you wear,
That th' eyes of busy fools may be stopp'd there.
Unlace yourself, for that harmonious chime
Tells me from you that now it is bed-time.
Off with that happy busk, which I envy,
That still can be, and still can stand so nigh.
Your gown going off such beauteous state reveals,
As when from flowery meads th' hill's shadow steals.
Off with your wiry coronet, and show
The hairy diadem which on you doth grow.
Off with your hose and shoes; then softly tread
In this love's hallow'd temple, this soft bed.
In such white robes heaven's angels used to be
Revealed to men; thou, angel, bring'st with thee
A heaven-like Mahomet's paradise; and though
Ill spirits walk in white, we easily know
By this these angels from an evil sprite;
Those set our hairs, but these our flesh upright.

Licence my roving hands, and let them go
Before, behind, between, above, below.
O, my America, my Newfoundland,
My kingdom, safest when with one man mann'd,
My mine of precious stones, my empery;

How blest am I in this discovering thee!
To enter in these bonds, is to be free;
Then, where my hand is set, my seal shall be.

Full nakedness ! All joys are due to thee;
As souls unbodied, bodies unclothed must be
To taste whole joys. Gems which you women use
Are like Atlanta's ball cast in men's views;
That, when a fool's eye lighteth on a gem,
His earthly soul may covert theirs, not them:
Like pictures, or like books' gay coverings made
For laymen, are all women thus array'd.
Themselves are mystic books, which only we
—Whom their imputed grace will dignify—
Must see reveal'd. Then, since that I may know,
As liberally as to thy midwife show
Thyself; cast all, yea, this white linen hence;
There is no penance much less innocence:
To teach thee, I am naked first; why then,
What needst thou have more covering than a man?

John Donne

Go, Lovely Rose

Go, lovely rose!
Tell her that wastes her time and me,
That now she knows,
When I resemble her to thee,
How sweet and fair she seems to be.

Tell her that's young,
And shuns to have her graces spied,
That hadst thou sprung
In deserts where no men abide,
Thou must have uncommended died.

Small is the worth
Of beauty from the light retired;
Bid her come forth,
Suffer herself to be desired,
And not blush so to be admired.

Then die! that she
The common fate of all things rare
May read in thee;
How small a part of time they share
That are so wondrous sweet and fair.

Edmund Waller

Cherry-Ripe

There is a garden in her face
  Where roses and white lilies grow;
A heavenly paradise is that place,
  Wherein all pleasant fruits do flow:
  There cherries grow which none may buy
  Till 'Cherry-ripe' themselves do cry.

Those cherries fairly do enclose
  Of orient pearl a double row,
Which when her lovely laughter shows,
  They look like rose-buds fill'd with snow;
  Yet them nor peer nor prince can buy
  Till 'Cherry-ripe' themselves do cry.

Her eyes like angels watch them still;
  Her brows like bended bows do stand,
Threat'ning with piercing frowns to kill
  All that attempt with eye or hand
  Those sacred cherries to come nigh,
  Till 'Cherry-ripe' themselves do cry.

Thomas Campion

She Dwelt Among the Untrodden Ways

(an extract from *Lucy*)

She dwelt among the untrodden ways
Beside the springs of Dove,
A Maid whom there were none to praise,
And very few to love.

A Violet by a mossy stone
Half-hidden from the eye!
—Fair as a star, when only one
Is shining in the sky.

She lived unknown, and few could know
When Lucy ceased to be;
But she is in her Grave, and, oh,
The difference to me!

William Wordsworth

I Sing

I sing to use the waiting
My bonnet but to tie,
And close the door unto my house
No more to do have I.

'Till his best step approaching,
We journey to the day,
And tell each other how we sung
To keep the dark away.

Emily Dickinson

Sweet Disorder

A sweet disorder in the dress
Kindles in clothes a wantonness:
A lawn about the shoulders thrown
Into a fine distraction—
An erring lace, which here and there
Enthrals the crimson stomacher—
A cuff neglectful, and thereby
Ribbands to flow confusedly—
A winning wave, deserving note,
In the tempestuous petticoat—
A careless shoe-string, in whose tie
I see a wild civility—
Do more bewitch me than when art
Is too precise in every part.

Robert Herrick

She Walks in Beauty

She walks in beauty, like the night
Of cloudless climes and starry skies;
And all that's best of dark and bright
Meet in her aspect and her eyes:
Thus mellowed to that tender light
Which heaven to gaudy day denies.

One shade the more, one ray the less,
Had half impaired the nameless grace
Which waves in every raven tress,
Or softly lightens o'er her face;
Where thoughts serenely sweet express
How pure, how dear their dwelling-place.

And on that cheek, and o'er that brow,
So soft, so calm, yet eloquent,
The smiles that win, the tints that glow,
But tell of days in goodness spent,
A mind at peace with all below,
A heart whose love is innocent!

George Gordon, Lord Byron

Love's Philosophy

The fountains mingle with the river
And the rivers with the ocean,
The winds of heaven mix for ever
With a sweet emotion;
Nothing in the world is single,
All things by a law divine
In one another's being mingle—
Why not I with thine?

See the mountains kiss high heaven
And the waves clasp one another;
No sister-flower would be forgiven
If it disdain'd its brother:
And the sunlight clasps the earth,
And the moonbeams kiss the sea—
What are all these kissings worth,
If thou kiss not me?

Percy Bysshe Shelley

One Day I Wrote Her Name Upon the Strand

One day I wrote her name upon the strand,
But came the waves and washed it away:
Again I wrote it with a second hand,
But came the tide, and made my pains his prey.
Vain man, said she, that dost in vain assay
A mortal thing so to immortalize!
For I myself shall like to this decay,
And eke my name be wiped out likewise.
Not so quoth I, let baser things devise
To die in dust, but you shall live by fame:
My verse your virtues rare shall eternize,
And in the heavens write your glorious name;
Where, whenas death shall all the world subdue,
Our love shall live, and later life renew.

Edmund Spenser

The Good-Morrow

I wonder, by my troth, what thou and I
Did, till we loved? Were we not weaned till then?
But sucked on country pleasures, childishly?
Or snorted we in the seven sleepers' den?
'Twas so; but this, all pleasures fancies be.
If ever any beauty I did see,
Which I desired, and got, 'twas but a dream of thee.

And now good-morrow to our waking souls,
Which watch not one another out of fear;
For love, all love of other sights controls,
And makes one little room an everywhere.
Let sea-discoverers to new worlds have gone,
Let maps to other, worlds on worlds have shown,
Let us possess one world, each hath one, and is one.

My face in thine eye, thine in mine appears,
And true plain hearts do in the faces rest;
Where can we find two better hemispheres
Without sharp North, without declining West?
Whatever dies was not mixed equally;
If our two loves be one, or thou and I
Love so alike that none do slacken, none can die.

John Donne

Sonnet 18: Shall I compare thee to a summer's day?

Shall I compare thee to a summer's day?
  Thou art more lovely and more temperate:
Rough winds do shake the darling buds of May,
  And summer's lease hath all too short a date:
Sometime too hot the eye of heaven shines,
  And often is his gold complexion dimm'd;
And every fair from fair sometime declines,
  By chance, or nature's changing course, untrimm'd;
But thy eternal summer shall not fade,
  Nor lose possession of that fair thou owest;
Nor shall Death brag thou wander'st in his shade,
  When in eternal lines to time thou growest;
So long as men can breathe, or eyes can see,
  So long lives this, and this gives life to thee.

William Shakespeare

Sonnets from the Portuguese: 13

And wilt thou have me fashion into speech
The love I bear thee, finding words enough,
And hold the torch out, while the winds are rough,
Between our faces, to cast light on each?
I drop it at thy feet. I cannot teach
My hand to hold my spirit so far off
From myself—me—that I should bring thee proof
In words, of love hid in me out of reach.
Nay, let the silence of my womanhood
Commend my woman-love to thy belief,—
Seeing that I stand unwon, however wooed,
And rend the garment of my life, in brief,
By a most dauntless, voiceless fortitude,
Lest one touch of this heart convey its grief.

Elizabeth Barrett Browning

Two Lovers

Two lovers by a moss-grown spring:
They leaned soft cheeks together there,
Mingled the dark and sunny hair,
And heard the wooing thrushes sing.
O budding time!
O love's blest prime!

Two wedded from the portal stept:
The bells made happy carolings,
The air was soft as fanning wings,
White petals on the pathway slept.
O pure-eyed bride!
O tender pride!

Two faces o'er a cradle bent:
Two hands above the head were locked:
These pressed each other while they rocked,
Those watched a life that love had sent.
O solemn hour!
O hidden power!

Two parents by the evening fire:
The red light fell about their knees
On heads that rose by slow degrees
Like buds upon the lily spire.
O patient life!
O tender strife!

The two still sat together there,
The red light shone about their knees;

But all the heads by slow degrees
Had gone and left that lonely pair.
O voyage fast!
O vanished past!

The red light shone upon the floor
And made the space between them wide;
They drew their chairs up side by side,
Their pale cheeks joined, and said, "Once more!"
O memories!
O past that is!

George Eliot

The Kiss

I hoped that he would love me,
And he has kissed my mouth,
But I am like a stricken bird
That cannot reach the south.
For though I know he loves me,
To-night my heart is sad;
His kiss was not so wonderful
As all the dreams I had.

Sara Teasdale

The Clod and the Pebble

'Love seeketh not itself to please,
  Nor for itself hath any care,
But for another gives its ease,
  And builds a heaven in hell's despair.'

So sung a little clod of clay,
  Trodden with the cattle's feet,
But a pebble of the brook
  Warbled out these metres meet:

'Love seeketh only Self to please,
  To bind another to its delight,
Joys in another's loss of ease,
  And builds a hell in heaven's despite.'

William Blake

The Sun Rising

Busy old fool, unruly Sun,
　Why dost thou thus,
Through windows, and through curtains, call on us?
Must to thy motions lovers' seasons run?
　Saucy pedantic wretch, go chide
　Late school-boys and sour prentices,
　Go tell court-huntsmen that the king will ride,
　Call country ants to harvest offices;
Love, all alike, no season knows nor clime,
Nor hours, days, months, which are the rags of time.

Thy beams so reverend, and strong
　Why shouldst thou think?
I could eclipse and cloud them with a wink,
But that I would not lose her sight so long.
　If her eyes have not blinded thine,
　Look, and to-morrow late tell me,
　Whether both th' Indias of spice and mine
　Be where thou left'st them, or lie here with me.
Ask for those kings whom thou saw'st yesterday,
And thou shalt hear, 'All here in one bed lay.'

She's all states, and all princes, I;
　Nothing else is;
Princes do but play us; compared to this,
All honour's mimic, all wealth alchemy.
　Thou, Sun, art half as happy as we,
　In that the world's contracted thus;
　Thine age asks ease, and since thy duties be
　To warm the world, that's done in warming us.

Shine here to us, and thou art everywhere;
This bed thy center is, these walls thy sphere.

John Donne

You Smiled, You Spoke And I Believed

You smiled, you spoke and I believed,
By every word and smile—deceived.
Another man would hope no more;
Nor hope I—what I hoped before.
But let not this last wish be vain;
Deceive, deceive me once again!

Walter Savage Landor

The Definition of Love

My Love is of a birth as rare
  As 'tis, for object, strange and high;
It was begotten by Despair,
  Upon Impossibility.

Magnanimous Despair alone
  Could show me so divine a thing,
Where feeble hope could ne'er have flown,
  But vainly flapped its tinsel wing.

And yet I quickly might arrive
  Where my extended soul is fixed;
But Fate does iron wedges drive,
  And always crowds itself betwixt.

For Fate with jealous eye does see
  Two perfect loves, nor lets them close;
Their union would her ruin be,
  And her tyrannic power depose.

And therefore her decrees of steel
  Us as the distant poles have placed,
(Though Love's whole world on us doth wheel),
  Not by themselves to be embraced,

Unless the giddy heaven fall,
  And earth some new convulsion tear.
And, us to join, the world should all
  Be cramp'd into a planisphere.

As lines, so Love's oblique, may well
   Themselves in every angle greet:
But ours, so truly parallel,
   Though infinite, can never meet.

Therefore the Love which us doth bind,
   But Fate so enviously debars,
Is the conjunction of the mind,
   And opposition of the stars.

Andrew Marvell

That I Did Always Love

That I did always love
I bring thee Proof
That till I loved
I never lived—Enough—

That I shall love alway—
I argue thee
That love is life—
And life hath Immortality—

This—dost thou doubt—Sweet—
Then have I
Nothing to show
But Calvary—

Emily Dickinson

To Lucasta, on Going to the Wars

Tell me not, Sweet, I am unkind
For, from the nunnery
Of thy chaste breast, and quiet mind,
To war and arms I fly.

True, a new mistress now I chase,
The first foe in the field;
And with a stronger faith embrace
A sword, a horse, a shield.

Yet this unconstancy is such
As you too shall adore;
For, I could not love thee, Dear, so much,
Loved I not honour more.

Richard Lovelace

The Silent Lover I

Passions are liken'd best to floods and streams:
The shallow murmur, but the deep are dumb;
So, when affection yields discourse, it seems
The bottom is but shallow whence they come.
They that are rich in words, in words discover
That they are poor in that which makes a lover.

Sir Walter Raleigh

Love Song

When my soul touches yours a great chord sings!
How shall I tune it then to other things?
O! That some spot in darkness could be found
That does not vibrate whene'er your depth sound.
But everything that touches you and me
Welds us as played strings sound one melody.
Where is the instrument whence the sounds flow?
And whose the master-hand that holds the bow?
O! Sweet song—

Rainer Maria Rilke (tr. Jessie Lemont)

A Glimpse

A glimpse through an interstice caught,
Of a crowd of workmen and drivers in a bar-room
  around the stove late of a winter night, and I
  unremark'd seated in a corner,
Of a youth who loves me and whom I love, silently
  approaching and seating himself near, that he may
  hold me by the hand,
A long while amid the noises of coming and going, of
  drinking and oath and smutty jest,
There we two, content, happy in being together,
  speaking little, perhaps not a word.

Walt Whitman

To Celia

Drink to me only with thine eyes,
   And I will pledge with mine;
Or leave a kiss but in the cup
   And I'll not look for wine.
The thirst that from the soul doth rise
   Doth ask a drink divine;
But might I of Jove's nectar sup,
   I would not change for thine.

I sent thee late a rosy wreath,
   Not so much honouring thee
As giving it a hope that there
   It could not wither'd be;
But thou thereon didst only breathe,
   And sent'st it back to me;
Since when it grows, and smells, I swear,
   Not of itself but thee!

Ben Jonson

Severed Selves

Two separate divided silences,
Which, brought together, would find loving voice;
Two glances which together would rejoice
In love, now lost like stars beyond dark trees;
Two hands apart whose touch alone gives ease;
Two bosoms which, heart-shrined with mutual flame,
Would, meeting in one clasp, be made the same;
Two souls, the shores wave-mocked of sundering seas:—
Such are we now. Ah! may our hope forecast
Indeed one hour again, when on this stream
Of darkened love once more the light shall gleam?—
An hour how slow to come, how quickly past,—
Which blooms and fades, and only leaves at last,
Faint as shed flowers, the attenuated dream.

Dante Gabriel Rossetti

Love's Secret

Never seek to tell thy love,
  Love that never told can be;
For the gentle wind doth move
  Silently, invisibly.
I told my love, I told my love,
  I told her all my heart,
Trembling, cold, in ghastly fears.
  Ah! she did depart!

Soon after she was gone from me,
  A traveller came by,
Silently, invisibly:
  He took her with a sigh.

William Blake

As if a Phantom Caress'd Me

As if a phantom caress'd me,
I thought I was not alone walking here by the shore;
But the one I thought was with me as now I walk by
    the shore, the one I loved that caress'd me,
As I lean and look through the glimmering light, that
    one has utterly disappear'd,
And those appear that are hateful to me and mock me.

Walt Whitman

Song of the Statue

Who so loveth me that he
Will give his precious life for me?
I shall be set free from the stone
If some one drowns for me in the sea,
I shall have life, life of my own,—
For life I ache.

I long for the singing blood,
The stone is so still and cold.
I dream of life, life is good.
Will no one love me and be bold
And me awake?

* * *

I weep and weep alone,
Weep always for my stone.
What joy is my blood to me
If it ripens like red wine?
It cannot call back from the sea
The life that was given for mine,
Given for Love's sake.

Rainer Maria Rilke (tr. Jessie Lemont)

A Moment

The clouds had made a crimson crown
  About the mountains high.
The stormy sun was going down
  In a stormy sky.

Why did you let your eyes so rest on me,
  And hold your breath between?
In all the ages this can never be
  As if it had not been.

Mary Elizabeth Coleridge

Love-Free

I am free of love as a bird flying south in the autumn,
Swift and intent, asking no joy from another,
Glad to forget all of the passion of April
Ere it was love-free.
I am free of love, and I listen to music lightly,
But if he returned, if he should look at me deeply,
I should awake, I should awake and remember
I am my lover's.

Sara Teasdale

To my Inconstant Mistress

When thou, poor excommunicate
From all the joys of love, shalt see
The full reward and glorious fate
Which my strong faith shall purchase me,
Then curse thine own inconstancy.

A fairer hand than thine shall cure
That heart which thy false oaths did wound;
And to my soul a soul more pure
Than thine shall by Love's hand be bound,
And both with equal glory crowned.
Then shalt thou weep, entreat, complain
To Love, as I did once to thee;
When all thy tears shall be as vain
As mine were then, for thou shalt be
Damned for thy false apostasy.

Thomas Carew

The Appeal

And wilt thou leave me thus!
Say nay, say nay, for shame!
—To save thee from the blame
Of all my grief and grame.
And wilt thou leave me thus?
    Say nay! say nay!

And wilt thou leave me thus,
That hath loved thee so long
In wealth and woe among:
And is thy heart so strong
As for to leave me thus?
    Say nay! say nay!

And wilt thou leave me thus,
That hath given thee my heart
Never for to depart
Neither for pain nor smart:
And wilt thou leave me thus?
    Say nay! say nay!

And wilt thou leave me thus,
And have no more pitye
Of him that loveth thee?
Alas, thy cruelty!
And wilt thou leave me thus?
    Say nay! say nay!

Sir Thomas Wyatt

His Lady's Cruelty

With how sad steps, O moon, thou climb'st the skies!
How silently, and with how wan a face!
What! may it be that even in heavenly place
That busy archer his sharp arrows tries?
Sure, if that long-with-love-acquainted eyes
Can judge of love, thou feel'st a lover's case:
I read it in thy looks; thy languish'd grace
To me, that feel the like, thy state descries.
Then, even of fellowship, O moon, tell me,
Is constant love deem'd there but want of wit?
Are beauties there as proud as here they be?
Do they above love to be loved, and yet
   Those lovers scorn whom that love doth possess?
   Do they call 'virtue' there—ungratefulness?

Sir Philip Sidney

Fast Anchor'd, Eternal, O Love!

Fast-anchor'd, eternal, O love! O woman I love!
O bride! O wife! more resistless than I can tell, the
   thought of you!
Then separate, as disembodied or another born,
Ethereal, the last athletic reality, my consolation,
I ascend, I float in the regions of your love O man,
O sharer of my roving life.

Walt Whitman

Pretty Twinkling Starry Eyes

Pretty twinkling starry eyes,
How did Nature first devise
Such a sparkling in your sight
As to give Love such delight,
As to make him like a fly,
Play with looks until he die?

Sure ye were not made at first
For such mischief to be curst;
As to kill Affection's care
That doth only truth declare;
Where worth's wonders never wither,
Love and Beauty live together.

Blessed eyes, then give your blessing,
That in passion's best expressing;
Love that only lives to grace ye,
May not suffer pride deface ye;
But in gentle thought's directions
Show the power of your perfections.

Nicholas Breton

Carrier Letter

My hands have not touched water since your hands,—
No;—nor my lips freed laughter since 'farewell'.
And with the day, distance again expands
Between us, voiceless as an uncoiled shell.

Yet,—much follows, much endures... Trust birds alone:
A dove's wings clung about my heart last night
With surging gentleness; and the blue stone
Set in the tryst-ring has but worn more bright.

Hart Crane

Sonnet 116: Let me not to the marriage of true minds

Let me not to the marriage of true minds
Admit impediments. Love is not love
Which alters when it alteration finds,
Or bends with the remover to remove:
O no! it is an ever-fixed mark
That looks on tempests and is never shaken;
It is the star to every wandering bark,
Whose worth's unknown, although his height be taken.
Love's not Time's fool, though rosy lips and cheeks
Within his bending sickle's compass come:
Love alters not with his brief hours and weeks,
But bears it out even to the edge of doom.
  If this be error and upon me proved,
  I never writ, nor no man ever loved.

William Shakespeare

To His Coy Mistress

Had we but world enough, and time,
This coyness, lady, were no crime.
We would sit down and think which way
To walk, and pass our long love's day;
Thou by the Indian Ganges' side
Shouldst rubies find; I by the tide
Of Humber would complain. I would
Love you ten years before the Flood;
And you should, if you please, refuse
Till the conversion of the Jews.
My vegetable love should grow
Vaster than empires, and more slow.
An hundred years should go to praise
Thine eyes, and on thy forehead gaze;
Two hundred to adore each breast,
But thirty thousand to the rest;
An age at least to every part,
And the last age should show your heart.
For, lady, you deserve this state,
Nor would I love at lower rate.

But at my back I always hear
Time's winged chariot hurrying near;
And yonder all before us lie
Deserts of vast eternity.
Thy beauty shall no more be found,
Nor, in thy marble vault, shall sound
My echoing song; then worms shall try
That long preserv'd virginity,
And your quaint honour turn to dust,

And into ashes all my lust.
The grave's a fine and private place,
But none I think do there embrace.

Now therefore, while the youthful hue
Sits on thy skin like morning dew,
And while thy willing soul transpires
At every pore with instant fires,
Now let us sport us while we may;
And now, like am'rous birds of prey,
Rather at once our time devour,
Than languish in his slow-chapp'd power.
Let us roll all our strength, and all
Our sweetness, up into one ball;
And tear our pleasures with rough strife
Thorough the iron gates of life.
Thus, though we cannot make our sun
Stand still, yet we will make him run.

Andrew Marvell

Silent Noon

Your hands lie open in the long fresh grass,—
The finger-points look through like rosy blooms:
Your eyes smile peace. The pasture gleams and glooms
'Neath billowing skies that scatter and amass.
All round our nest, far as the eye can pass,
Are golden kingcup-fields with silver edge
Where the cow-parsley skirts the hawthorn-hedge.
'Tis visible silence, still as the hour-glass.
Deep in the sun-searched growths the dragon-fly
Hangs like a blue thread loosened from the sky:—
So this wing'd hour is dropt to us from above.
Oh! clasp we to our hearts, for deathless dower,
This close-companioned inarticulate hour
When twofold silence was the song of love.

Dante Gabriel Rossetti

To A Stranger

Passing stranger! you do not know how longingly I look
    upon you,
You must be he I was seeking, or she I was seeking, (it
    comes to me as of a dream,)
I have somewhere surely lived a life of joy with you,
All is recall'd as we flit by each other, fluid, affectionate,
    chaste, matured,
You grew up with me, were a boy with me or a girl
    with me,
I ate with you and slept with you, your body has
    become not yours only nor left my body mine only,
You give me the pleasure of your eyes, face, flesh, as we
    pass, you take of my beard, breast, hands, in return,
I am not to speak to you, I am to think of you when I
    sit alone or wake at night alone,
I am to wait, I do not doubt I am to meet you again,
I am to see to it that I do not lose you.

Walt Whitman

The Silent Lover II

Wrong not, sweet empress of my heart,
    The merit of true passion,
With thinking that he feels no smart,
    That sues for no compassion.

Silence in love bewrays more woe
    Than words, though ne'er so witty:
A beggar that is dumb, you know,
    May challenge double pity.

Then wrong not, dearest to my heart,
    My true, though secret passion;
He smarteth most that hides his smart,
    And sues for no compassion.

Sir Walter Raleigh

Those Who Love

Those who love the most,
Do not talk of their love,
Francesca, Guinevere,
Deirdre, Iseult, Heloise,
In the fragrant gardens of heaven
Are silent, or speak if at all
Of fragile, inconsequent things.

And a woman I used to know
Who loved one man from her youth,
Against the strength of the fates
Fighting in somber pride,
Never spoke of this thing,
But hearing his name by chance,
A light would pass over her face.

Sara Teasdale

The Night Piece: To Julia

Her eyes the glow-worm lend thee,
The shooting stars attend thee;
And the elves also,
Whose little eyes glow
Like the sparks of fire, befriend thee.

No Will-o'-th'-Wisp mis-light thee,
Nor snake or slow-worm bite thee;
But on, on thy way,
Not making a stay,
Since ghost there's none to affright thee.

Let not the dark thee cumber;
What though the moon does slumber?
The stars of the night
Will lend thee their light,
Like tapers clear without number.

Then Julia let me woo thee,
Thus, thus to come unto me;
And when I shall meet
Thy silv'ry feet,
My soul I'll pour into thee.

Robert Herrick

Sonnet 147: My love is as a fever, longing still

My love is as a fever, longing still
For that which longer nurseth the disease,
Feeding on that which doth preserve the ill,
Th' uncertain sickly appetite to please.
My reason, the physician to my love,
Angry that his prescriptions are not kept,
Hath left me, and I desperate now approve
Desire is death, which physic did except.
Past cure I am, now reason is past care,
And frantic-mad with evermore unrest;
My thoughts and my discourse as madmen's are,
At random from the truth vainly expressed:
  For I have sworn thee fair, and thought thee bright,
  Who art as black as hell, as dark as night.

William Shakespeare

Desire

Where true Love burns Desire is Love's pure flame;
It is the reflex of our earthly frame,
That takes its meaning from the nobler part,
And but translates the language of the heart.

Samuel Taylor Coleridge

At the Mid Hour of Night

At the mid hour of night, when stars are weeping, I fly
To the lone vale we lov'd, when life shone warm in
  thine eye;
And I think oft, if spirits can steal from the regions of
  air,
To revisit past scenes of delight, thou wilt come to me
  there,
And tell me our love is remember'd, ev'n in the sky.

Then I sing the wild song, 'twas once such rapture to
  hear
When our voices commingling, breath'd like one on the
  ear;
And, as echo far off through the vale my sad orison
  rolls,
I think, oh my love! 'tis thy voice from the kingdom of
  souls
Faintly answering still the notes that once were so dear.

Thomas Moore

The First Day

I wish I could remember the first day,
First hour, first moment of your meeting me,
If bright or dim the season, it might be
Summer or winter for aught I can say;
So unrecorded did it slip away,
So blind was I to see and to foresee,
So dull to mark the budding of my tree
That would not blossom, yet, for many a May.
If only I could recollect it. Such
A day of days! I let it come and go
As traceless as a thaw of bygone snow;
It seemed to mean so little, meant so much;
If only now I could recall that touch,
First touch of hand in hand—Did one, but know!

Christina Georgina Rossetti

Bright Star

Bright star, would I were steadfast as thou art—
  Not in lone splendour hung aloft the night
And watching, with eternal lids apart,
  Like nature's patient, sleepless Eremite,
The moving waters at their priestlike task
  Of pure ablution round earth's human shores,
Or gazing on the new soft-fallen mask
  Of snow upon the mountains and the moors—
No—yet still steadfast, still unchangeable,
  Pillow'd upon my fair love's ripening breast,
To feel for ever its soft fall and swell,
  Awake for ever in a sweet unrest,
Still, still to hear her tender-taken breath,
  And so live ever—or else swoon to death.

John Keats

Strange Fits of Passion Have I Known

Strange fits of passion have I known:
And I will dare to tell,
But in the Lover's ear alone,
What once to me befell.

When she I loved looked every day
Fresh as a rose in June,
I to her cottage bent my way,
Beneath an evening moon.

Upon the moon I fixed my eye,
All over the wide lea;
With quickening pace my horse drew nigh
Those paths so dear to me.

And now we reached the orchard-plot;
And, as we climbed the hill,
The sinking moon to Lucy's cot
Came near, and nearer still.

In one of those sweet dreams I slept,
Kind Nature's gentlest boon!
And all the while my eyes I kept
On the descending moon.

My horse moved on; hoof after hoof
He raised, and never stopped:
When down behind the cottage roof,
At once, the bright moon dropped.

What fond and wayward thoughts will slide
Into a Lover's head!
'O mercy!' to myself I cried,
'If Lucy should be dead!'

William Wordsworth

Madonna of the Evening Flowers

All day long I have been working
Now I am tired.
I call: "Where are you?"
But there is only the oak tree rustling in the wind.
The house is very quiet,
The sun shines in on your books,
On your scissors and thimble just put down,
But you are not there.
Suddenly I am lonely:
Where are you?
I go about searching.

Then I see you,
Standing under a spire of pale blue larkspur,
With a basket of roses on your arm.
You are cool, like silver,
And you smile.
I think the Canterbury bells are playing little tunes,
You tell me that the peonies need spraying,
That the columbines have overrun all bounds,
That the pyrus japonica should be cut back and
    rounded.

You tell me these things.
But I look at you, heart of silver,
White heart-flame of polished silver,
Burning beneath the blue steeples of the larkspur,
And I long to kneel instantly at your feet,
While all about us peal the loud, sweet Te Deums of the
    Canterbury bells.

Amy Lowell

Marriage

No more alone sleeping, no more alone waking,
Thy dreams divided, thy prayers in twain;
Thy merry sisters tonight forsaking,
Never shall we see, maiden, again.

Never shall we see thee, thine eyes glancing.
Flashing with laughter and wild in glee,
Under the mistletoe kissing and dancing,
Wantonly free.

There shall come a matron walking sedately,
Low-voiced, gentle, wise in reply.
Tell me, O tell me, can I love her greatly?
All for her sake must the maiden die!

Mary Elizabeth Coleridge

Helas

To drift with every passion till my soul
Is a stringed lute on which all winds can play,
Is it for this that I have given away
Mine ancient wisdom, and austere control?
Methinks my life is a twice-written scroll
Scrawled over on some boyish holiday
With idle songs for pipe and virelay,
Which do but mar the secret of the whole.
Surely there was a time I might have trod
The sunlit heights, and from life's dissonance
Struck one clear chord to reach the ears of God:
Is that time dead? lo! with a little rod
I did but touch the honey of romance—
And must I lose a soul's inheritance?

Oscar Wilde

I Love You

When April bends above me
And finds me fast asleep
Dust need not keep the secret
A live heart died to keep.
When April tells the thrushes,
The meadow-larks will know,
And pipe the three words lightly
To all the winds that blow.
Above his roof the swallows,
In notes like far-blown rain,
Will tell the little sparrow
Beside his window-pane.
O sparrow, little sparrow,
When I am fast asleep,
Then tell my love the secret
That I have died to keep.

Sara Teasdale

False though She be

False though she be to me and love,
   I'll ne'er pursue revenge;
For still the charmer I approve,
   Though I deplore her change.

In hours of bliss we oft have met:
   They could not always last;
And though the present I regret,
   I'm grateful for the past.

William Congreve

Sonnet 130: My mistress' eyes
are nothing like the sun

My mistress' eyes are nothing like the sun;
   Coral is far more red than her lips' red;
If snow be white, why then her breasts are dun;
   If hairs be wires, black wires grow on her head.

I have seen roses damask'd, red and white,
   But no such roses see I in her cheeks;
And in some perfumes is there more delight
   Than in the breath that from my mistress reeks.

I love to hear her speak, yet well I know
   That music hath a far more pleasing sound;
I grant I never saw a goddess go;
   My mistress, when she walks, treads on the ground.
And yet, by heaven, I think my love as rare
   As any she belied with false compare.

William Shakespeare

Without Her

What of her glass without her? The blank grey
There where the pool is blind of the moon's face.
Her dress without her? The tossed empty space
Of cloud-rack when the moon has passed away.
Her paths without her? Day's appointed sway
Usurped by desolate night. Her pillowed place
Without her? Tears, ah me! For love's good grace,
And cold forgetfulness of night or day.

What of the heart without her? Nay, poor heart,
Of thee what word remains ere speech be still?
A wayfarer by barren ways and chill,
Steep ways and weary, without her thou art,
Where the long cloud, the long wood's counterpart,
Sheds doubled darkness up the labouring hill.

Dante Gabriel Rossetti

Song

Go and catch a falling star,
Get with child a mandrake root,
Tell me where all past years are,
Or who cleft the devil's foot,
Teach me to hear mermaids singing,
Or to keep off envy's stinging,
   And find
   What wind
Serves to advance an honest mind.

If thou be'st born to strange sights,
Things invisible to see,
Ride ten thousand days and nights,
Till age snow white hairs on thee,
Thou, when thou return'st, wilt tell me,
All strange wonders that befell thee,
   And swear,
   No where
Lives a woman true and fair.

If thou find'st one, let me know,
Such a pilgrimage were sweet;
Yet do not, I would not go,
Though at next door we might meet,

Though she were true, when you met her,
And last, till you write your letter,
  Yet she
  Will be
False, ere I come, to two, or three.

John Donne

Ruth

She stood breast-high amid the corn,
Clasp'd by the golden light of morn,
Like the sweetheart of the sun,
Who many a glowing kiss had won.

On her cheek an autumn flush,
Deeply ripen'd;—such a blush
In the midst of brown was born,
Like red poppies grown with corn.

Round her eyes her tresses fell,
Which were blackest none could tell,
But long lashes veil'd a light,
That had else been all too bright.

And her hat, with shady brim,
Made her tressy forehead dim;
Thus she stood amid the stooks,
Praising God with sweetest looks:–

Sure, I said, Heav'n did not mean,
Where I reap thou shouldst but glean,
Lay thy sheaf adown and come,
Share my harvest and my home.

Thomas Hood

To Sylvia, To Wed

Let us, though late, at last, my Silvia, wed;
And loving lie in one devoted bed.
Thy watch may stand, my minutes fly post haste;
No sound calls back the year that once is past.
Then, sweetest Silvia, let's no longer stay;
True love, we know, precipitates delay.
Away with doubts, all scruples hence remove!
No man, at one time, can be wise, and love.

Robert Herrick

Delia XXXI: Look, Delia, how we esteem the half-blown rose,

Look, Delia, how we esteem the half-blown rose,
The image of thy blush, and summer's honour!
Whilst yet her tender bud doth undisclose
That full of beauty Time bestows upon her:
No sooner spreads her glory in the air,
But straight her wide-blown pomp comes to decline;
She then is scorn'd, that late adorn'd the fair.
So fade the roses of those cheeks of thine!
No April can revive thy withered flowers,
Whose springing grace adorns thy glory now:
Swift speedy Time, feathered with flying hours,
Dissolves the beauty of the fairest brow.
Then do not thou such treasure waste in vain,
But love now, whilst thou may'st be loved again.

Samuel Daniel

Down by the Salley Gardens

Down by the salley gardens my love and I did meet;
She passed the salley gardens with little snow-white
    feet.
She bid me take love easy, as the leaves grow on the
    tree;
But I, being young and foolish, with her would not
    agree.

In a field by the river my love and I did stand,
And on my leaning shoulder she laid her snow-white
    hand.
She bid me take life easy, as the grass grows on the
    weirs;
But I was young and foolish, and now am full of tears.

W. B. Yeats

The Bride

Call me, Beloved! Call aloud to me!
Thy bride her vigil at the window keeps;
The evening wanes to dusk, the dimness creeps
Down empty alleys of the old plane-tree.

O! Let thy voice enfold me close about,
Or from this dark house, lonely and remote,
Through deep blue gardens where gray shadows float
I will pour forth my soul with hands stretched out . . .

Rainer Maria Rilke (tr. Jessie Lemont)

Now Sleeps the Crimson Petal

Now sleeps the crimson petal, now the white;
Nor waves the cypress in the palace walk;
Nor winks the gold fin in the porphyry font:
The fire-fly wakens: waken thou with me.

Now droops the milkwhite peacock like a ghost,
And like a ghost she glimmers on to me.

Now lies the Earth all Danaë to the stars,
And all thy heart lies open unto me.
Now slides the silent meteor on, and leaves
A shining furrow, as thy thoughts in me.

Now folds the lily all her sweetness up,
And slips into the bosom of the lake:
So fold thyself, my dearest, thou, and slip
Into my bosom and be lost in me.

Alfred, Lord Tennyson

Farewell, Ungrateful Traitor!

Farewell, ungrateful traitor!
Farewell, my perjur'd swain!
Let never injur'd woman
Believe a man again.
The pleasure of possessing
Surpasses all expressing,
But 'tis too short a blessing,
And love too long a pain.

'Tis easy to deceive us
In pity of your pain,
But when we love, you leave us
To rail at you in vain.
Before we have descried it,
There is no joy beside it,
But she that once has tried it
Will never love again.

The passion you pretended
Was only to obtain,
But once the charm is ended,
The charmer you disdain.
Your love by ours we measure
Till we have lost our treasure,
But dying is a pleasure
When living is a pain.

John Dryden

A Broken Appointment

You did not come,
And marching Time drew on, and wore me numb.
Yet less for loss of your dear presence there
Than that I thus found lacking in your make
That high compassion which can overbear
Reluctance for pure loving kindness' sake
Grieved I, when, as the hope-hour stroked its sum,
You did not come.

You love not me,
And love alone can lend you loyalty;
—I know and knew it. But, unto the store
Of human deeds divine in all but name,
Was it not worth a little hour or more
To add yet this: Once you, a woman, came
To soothe a time-torn man; even though it be
You love not me?

Thomas Hardy

Elizabeth of Bohemia

You meaner beauties of the night,
    That poorly satisfy our eyes
More by your number than your light,
    You common people of the skies;
    What are you when the sun shall rise?

You curious chanters of the wood,
    That warble forth Dame Nature's lays,
Thinking your voices understood
    By your weak accents; what's your praise
    When Philomel her voice shall raise?

You violets that first appear,
    By your pure purple mantles known
Like the proud virgins of the year,
    As if the spring were all your own;
    What are you when the rose is blown?

So, when my mistress shall be seen
    In form and beauty of her mind,
By virtue first, then choice, a Queen,
    Tell me, if she were not design'd
    Th' eclipse and glory of her kind?

Sir Henry Wotton

To Mary Unwin

Mary! I want a lyre with other strings,
Such aid from Heaven as some have feign'd they drew,
An eloquence scarce given to mortals, new
And undebased by praise of meaner things;
That ere through age or woe I shed my wings,
I may record thy worth with honour due,
In verse as musical as thou art true,
And that immortalizes whom it sings:
But thou hast little need. There is a Book
By seraphs writ with beams of heavenly light,
On which the eyes of God not rarely look,
A chronicle of actions just and bright —
   There all thy deeds, my faithful Mary, shine;
   And since thou own'st that praise, I spare thee mine.

William Cowper

Renouncement

I must not think of thee; and, tired yet strong,
I shun the love that lurks in all delight—
The love of thee—and in the blue heaven's height,
And in the dearest passage of a song.
Oh, just beyond the sweetest thoughts that throng
This breast, the thought of thee waits hidden yet bright;
But it must never, never come in sight;
I must stop short of thee the whole day long.
But when sleep comes to close each difficult day,
When night gives pause to the long watch I keep,
And all my bonds I needs must loose apart,
Must doff my will as raiment laid away,—
With the first dream that comes with the first sleep
I run, I run, I am gather'd to thy heart.

Alice Meynell

Sweet Endings Come and Go, Love

La noche buena se viene,
La noche buena se va,
Y nosotros nos iremos
Y no volveremos mas.   OLD VILLANCICO

Sweet evenings come and go, love,
They came and went of yore:
This evening of our life, love,
Shall go and come no more.

When we have passed away, love,
All things will keep their name;
But yet no life on earth, love,
With ours will be the same.

The daisies will be there, love,
The stars in heaven will shine:
I shall not feel thy wish, love,
Nor thou my hand in thine.

A better time will come, love,
And better souls be born:
I would not be the best, love,
To leave thee now forlorn.

George Eliot

Love's Language

How does Love speak?
In the faint flush upon the telltale cheek,
And in the pallor that succeeds it; by
The quivering lid of an averted eye—
The smile that proves the parent to a sigh
Thus doth Love speak.

How does Love speak?
By the uneven heart-throbs, and the freak
Of bounding pulses that stand still and ache,
While new emotions, like strange barges, make
Along vein-channels their disturbing course;
Still as the dawn, and with the dawn's swift force—
Thus doth Love speak.

How does Love speak?
In the avoidance of that which we seek—
The sudden silence and reserve when near—
The eye that glistens with an unshed tear—
The joy that seems the counterpart of fear,
As the alarmèd heart leaps in the breast,
And knows, and names, and greets its godlike guest—
Thus doth Love speak.

How does Love speak?
In the proud spirit suddenly grown meek—
The haughty heart grown humble; in the tender
And unnamed light that floods the world with splendor;
In the resemblance which the fond eyes trace
In all fair things to one belovèd face;

In the shy touch of hands that thrill and tremble;
In looks and lips that can no more dissemble—
Thus doth Love speak.

How does Love speak?
In the wild words that uttered seem so weak
They shrink ashamed in silence; in the fire
Glance strikes with glance, swift flashing high and
  higher,
Like lightnings that precede the mighty storm;
In the deep, soulful stillness; in the warm,
Impassioned tide that sweeps through throbbing veins,
Between the shores of keen delights and pains;
In the embrace where madness melts in bliss,
And in the convulsive rapture of a kiss—
Thus doth Love speak.

Ella Wheeler Wilcox

Once I Pass'd Through a Populous City

Once I pass'd through a populous city imprinting my
   brain for future use with its shows, architecture,
   customs, traditions,
Yet now of all that city I remember only a woman I
   casually met there who detain'd me for love of me,
Day by day and night by night we were together—all
   else has long been forgotten by me,
I remember I say only that woman who passionately
   clung to me,
Again we wander, we love, we separate again,
Again she holds me by the hand, I must not go,
I see her close beside me with silent lips sad and
   tremulous.

Walt Whitman

Meeting at Night

The grey sea and the long black land;
And the yellow half-moon large and low;
And the startled little waves that leap
In fiery ringlets from their sleep,
As I gain the cove with pushing prow,
And quench its speed i' the slushy sand.

Then a mile of warm sea-scented beach;
Three fields to cross till a farm appears;
A tap at the pane, the quick sharp scratch
And blue spurt of a lighted match,
And a voice less loud, thro' its joys and fears,
Than the two hearts beating each to each!

Robert Browning

When We Two Parted

When we two parted
In silence and tears,
Half broken-hearted
To sever for years,
Pale grew thy cheek and cold,
Colder thy kiss;
Truly that hour foretold
Sorrow to this.

The dew of the morning
Sunk chill on my brow
It felt like the warning
Of what I feel now.
Thy vows are all broken,
And light is thy fame:
I hear thy name spoken,
And share in its shame.

They name thee before me,
A knell to mine ear;
A shudder comes o'er me
Why wert thou so dear?
They know not I knew thee,
Who knew thee too well:
Long, long shall I rue thee,
Too deeply to tell.

In secret we met,
In silence I grieve,
That thy heart could forget,

Thy spirit deceive.
If I should meet thee
After long years,
How should I greet thee?
With silence and tears.

George Gordon, Lord Byron

Echo

Come to me in the silence of the night;
    Come in the speaking silence of a dream;
Come with soft rounded cheeks and eyes as bright
    As sunlight on a stream;
        Come back in tears,
O memory, hope, love of finished years.

O dream how sweet, too sweet, too bitter sweet,
    Whose wakening should have been in Paradise,
Where souls brimfull of love abide and meet;
    Where thirsting longing eyes
        Watch the slow door
That opening, letting in, lets out no more.

Yet come to me in dreams, that I may live
    My very life again tho' cold in death:
Come back to me in dreams, that I may give
    Pulse for pulse, breath for breath:
        Speak low, lean low,
As long ago, my love, how long ago.

Christina Georgina Rossetti

The Ecstasy

Where, like a pillow on a bed,
  A pregnant bank swell'd up, to rest
The violet's reclining head,
  Sat we two, one another's best.

Our hands were firmly cemented
  With a fast balm, which thence did spring;
Our eye-beams twisted, and did thread
  Our eyes upon one double string.

So to intergraft our hands, as yet
  Was all the means to make us one;
And pictures in our eyes to get
  Was all our propagation.

As, 'twixt two equal armies, Fate
  Suspends uncertain victory,
Our souls—which to advance their state,
  Were gone out—hung 'twixt her and me.

And whilst our souls negotiate there,
  We like sepulchral statues lay;
All day, the same our postures were,
  And we said nothing, all the day.

If any, so by love refined,
   That he soul's language understood,
And by good love were grown all mind,
   Within convenient distance stood,

He—though he knew not which soul spake,
   Because both meant, both spake the same—
Might thence a new concoction take,
   And part far purer than he came.

This ecstasy doth unperplex
   (We said) and tell us what we love;
We see by this, it was not sex;
   We see, we saw not, what did move:

But as all several souls contain
   Mixture of things they know not what,
Love these mix'd souls doth mix again,
   And makes both one, each this, and that.

A single violet transplant,
   The strength, the colour, and the size—
All which before was poor and scant—
   Redoubles still, and multiplies.

When love with one another so
   Interanimates two souls,
That abler soul, which thence doth flow,
   Defects of loneliness controls.

We then, who are this new soul, know,
  Of what we are composed, and made,
For th' atomies of which we grow
  Are souls, whom no change can invade.

But, O alas! so long, so far,
  Our bodies why do we forbear?
They are ours, though not we; we are
  Th' intelligences, they the spheres.

We owe them thanks, because they thus
  Did us, to us, at first convey,
Yielded their forces, sense, to us,
  Nor are dross to us, but allay.

On man heaven's influence works not so,
  But that it first imprints the air;
So soul into the soul may flow,
  Though it to body first repair.

As our blood labours to beget
  Spirits, as like souls as it can;
Because such fingers need to knit
  That subtle knot, which makes us man;

So must pure lovers' souls descend
  To affections, and to faculties,
Which sense may reach and apprehend,
  Else a great prince in prison lies.

To our bodies turn we then, that so
  Weak men on love reveal'd may look;
Love's mysteries in souls do grow,
  But yet the body is his book.

And if some lover, such as we,
  Have heard this dialogue of one,
Let him still mark us, he shall see
  Small change when we're to bodies gone.

John Donne

Sonnets From The Portuguese: 14

If thou must love me, let it be for nought
Except for love's sake only. Do not say
I love her for her smile ... her look ... her way
Of speaking gently, ... for a trick of thought
That falls in well with mine, and certes brought
A sense of pleasant ease on such a day'—
For these things in themselves, Belovèd, may
Be changed, or change for thee,—and love, so wrought,
May be unwrought so. Neither love me for
Thine own dear pity's wiping my cheeks dry,—
A creature might forget to weep, who bore
Thy comfort long, and lose thy love thereby!
But love me for love's sake, that evermore
Thou may'st love on, through love's eternity.

Elizabeth Barrett Browning

The Indian Serenade

I arise from dreams of thee
In the first sweet sleep of night,
When the winds are breathing low,
And the stars are shining bright:
I arise from dreams of thee,
And a spirit in my feet
Hath led me—who knows how?
To thy chamber window, Sweet!

The wandering airs they faint
On the dark, the silent stream—
The Champak odours fail
Like sweet thoughts in a dream;
The Nightingale's complaint,
It dies upon her heart;—
As I must on thine,
Oh, belovèd as thou art!

Oh lift me from the grass!
I die! I faint! I fail!
Let thy love in kisses rain
On my lips and eyelids pale.
My cheek is cold and white, alas!
My heart beats loud and fast;—
Oh! press it to thine own again,
Where it will break at last.

Percy Bysshe Shelley

Sonnet 40: Take all my loves, my love, yea take them all

Take all my loves, my love, yea, take them all:
What hast thou then more than thou hadst before?
No love, my love, that thou mayst true love call—
All mine was thine before thou hadst this more.
Then if for my love thou my love receivest,
I cannot blame thee for my love thou usest;
But yet be blamed if thou this self deceivest
By wilful taste of what thyself refusest.
I do forgive thy robb'ry, gentle thief,
Although thou steal thee all my poverty;
And yet love knows it is a greater grief
To bear love's wrong than hate's known injury.
  Lascivious grace, in whom all ill well shows,
  Kill me with spites, yet we must not be foes.

William Shakespeare

I Loved You First: But Afterwards Your Love

Poca favilla gran fiamma seconda.—Dante

Ogni altra cosa, ogni pensier va fore,
E sol ivi con voi rimansi amore.—Petrarca

I loved you first: but afterwards your love
Outsoaring mine, sang such a loftier song
As drowned the friendly cooings of my dove.
Which owes the other most? my love was long,
And yours one moment seemed to wax more strong;
I loved and guessed at you, you construed me
And loved me for what might or might not be—
Nay, weights and measures do us both a wrong.
For verily love knows not 'mine' or 'thine;'
With separate 'I' and 'thou' free love has done,
For one is both and both are one in love:
Rich love knows nought of 'thine that is not mine;'
Both have the strength and both the length thereof,
Both of us, of the love which makes us one.

Christina Rossetti

Life In A Love

Escape me?
Never—
Beloved!
While I am I, and you are you,
So long as the world contains us both,
Me the loving and you the loth,
While the one eludes, must the other pursue.
My life is a fault at last, I fear:
It seems too much like a fate, indeed!
Though I do my best I shall scarce succeed.
But what if I fail of my purpose here?
It is but to keep the nerves at strain,
To dry one's eyes and laugh at a fall,
And, baffled, get up and begin again,—
So the chase takes up one's life, that's all.
While, look but once from your farthest bound
At me so deep in the dust and dark,
No sooner the old hope goes to ground
Than a new one, straight to the self-same mark,
I shape me—
Ever
Removed!

Robert Browning

Idea 61: Since there's no help, come let us kiss and part

Since there's no help, come let us kiss and part.
Nay, I have done, you get no more of me;
And I am glad, yea glad with all my heart,
That thus so cleanly I myself can free.
Shake hands for ever, cancel all our vows,
And when we meet at any time again,
Be it not seen in either of our brows
That we one jot of former love retain.
Now at the last gasp of Love's latest breath,
When, his pulse failing, Passion speechless lies;
When Faith is kneeling by his bed of death,
And Innocence is closing up his eyes—
Now, if thou wouldst, when all have given him over,
From death to life thou might'st him yet recover!

Michael Drayton

Love

All thoughts, all passions, all delights,
Whatever stirs this mortal frame,
All are but ministers of Love,
And feed his sacred flame.

Oft in my waking dreams do I
Live o'er again that happy hour,
When midway on the mount I lay,
Beside the ruined tower.

The moonshine, stealing o'er the scene
Had blended with the lights of eve;
And she was there, my hope, my joy,
My own dear Genevieve!

She leant against the armèd man,
The statue of the armèd Knight;
She stood and listened to my lay,
Amid the lingering light.

Few sorrows hath she of her own,
My hope! my joy! my Genevieve!
She loves me best, whene'er I sing
The songs that make her grieve.

I played a soft and doleful air,
I sang an old and moving story—
An old rude song, that suited well
That ruin wild and hoary.

She listened with a flitting blush,
With downcast eyes and modest grace;
For well she knew, I could not choose
But gaze upon her face.

I told her of the Knight that wore
Upon his shield a burning brand;
And that for ten long years he wooed
The Lady of the Land.

I told her how he pined: and ah!
The deep, the low, the pleading tone
With which I sang another's love,
Interpreted my own.

She listened with a flitting blush,
With downcast eyes, and modest grace;
And she forgave me, that I gazed
Too fondly on her face!

But when I told the cruel scorn
That crazed that bold and lovely Knight,
And that he crossed the mountain-woods,
Nor rested day nor night;

That sometimes from the savage den,
And sometimes from the darksome shade,
And sometimes starting up at once
In green and sunny glade,—

There came and looked him in the face
An angel beautiful and bright;

And that he knew it was a Fiend,
This miserable Knight!

And that unknowing what he did,
He leaped amid a murderous band,
And saved from outrage worse than death
The Lady of the Land!

And how she wept, and clasped his knees;
And how she tended him in vain—
And ever strove to expiate
The scorn that crazed his brain;—

And that she nursed him in a cave;
And how his madness went away,
When on the yellow forest-leaves
A dying man he lay;—

His dying words—but when I reached
That tenderest strain of all the ditty,
My faltering voice and pausing harp
Disturbed her soul with pity!

All impulses of soul and sense
Had thrilled my guileless Genevieve;
The music and the doleful tale,
The rich and balmy eve;

And hopes, and fears that kindle hope,
An undistinguishable throng,
And gentle wishes long subdued,
Subdued and cherished long!

She wept with pity and delight,
She blushed with love, and virgin-shame;
And like the murmur of a dream,
I heard her breathe my name.

Her bosom heaved—she stepped aside,
As conscious of my look she stepped—
Then suddenly, with timorous eye
She fled to me and wept.

She half enclosed me with her arms,
She pressed me with a meek embrace;
And bending back her head, looked up,
And gazed upon my face.

'Twas partly love, and partly fear,
And partly 'twas a bashful art,
That I might rather feel, than see,
The swelling of her heart.

I calmed her fears, and she was calm,
And told her love with virgin pride;
And so I won my Genevieve,
My bright and beauteous Bride.

Samuel Taylor Coleridge

To Mary

I sleep with thee, and wake with thee,
And yet thou art not there;
I fill my arms with thoughts of thee,
And press the common air,
Thy eyes are gazing upon mine,
When thou art out of sight;
My lips are always touching thine,
At morning, noon, and night.

I think and speak of other things
To keep my mind at rest;
But still to thee my memory clings
Like love in woman's breast.
I hide it from the world's wide eye,
And think and speak contrary;
But soft the wind comes from the sky,
And whispers tales of Mary.

The night wind whispers in my ear,
The moon shines in my face;
A burden still of chilling fear
I find in every place.
The breeze is whispering in the bush,
And the dews fall from the tree,
All sighing on, and will not hush,
Some pleasant tales of thee.

John Clare

The Apparition

When by thy scorne, O murdresse, I am dead,
And that thou thinkst thee free
From all solicitation from mee,
Then shall my ghost come to thy bed,
And thee, fain'd vestall, in worse armes shall see;
Then thy sicke taper will begin to winke,
And he, whose thou art then, being tyr'd before,
Will, if thou stirre, or pinch to wake him, thinke
    Thou call'st for more,
    And in false sleepe will from thee shrinke,
And then poore Aspen wretch, neglected thou
Bath'd in a cold quicksilver sweat wilt lye
    A veryer ghost than I;
    What I will say, I will not tell thee now,
    Lest that preserve thee; and since my love is spent,
I'had rather thou shouldst painfully repent,
Than by my threatenings rest still innocent.

John Donne

The Lover to His Lady

My girl, thou gazest much
  Upon the golden skies:
Would I were Heaven! I would behold
  Thee then with all mine eyes!

George Turberville

Annabel Lee

It was many and many a year ago,
   In a kingdom by the sea,
That a maiden there lived whom you may know
   By the name of Annabel Lee;
And this maiden she lived with no other thought
   Than to love and be loved by me.

I was a child and *she* was a child,
   In this kingdom by the sea,
But we loved with a love that was more than love—
   I and my Annabel Lee—
With a love that the wingèd seraphs of Heaven
   Coveted her and me.

And this was the reason that, long ago,
   In this kingdom by the sea,
A wind blew out of a cloud, chilling
   My beautiful Annabel Lee;
So that her highborn kinsmen came
   And bore her away from me,
To shut her up in a sepulchre
   In this kingdom by the sea.

The angels, not half so happy in Heaven,
   Went envying her and me—
Yes!—that was the reason (as all men know,
   In this kingdom by the sea)
That the wind came out of the cloud by night,
   Chilling and killing my Annabel Lee.

But our love it was stronger by far than the love
  Of those who were older than we—
  Of many far wiser than we—
And neither the angels in Heaven above
  Nor the demons down under the sea
Can ever dissever my soul from the soul
  Of the beautiful Annabel Lee;

For the moon never beams, without bringing me
  dreams
  Of the beautiful Annabel Lee;
And the stars never rise, but I feel the bright eyes
  Of the beautiful Annabel Lee;
And so, all the night-tide, I lie down by the side
  Of my darling—my darling—my life and my bride,
  In her sepulchre there by the sea—
  In her tomb by the sounding sea.

Edgar Allan Poe

To a Husband

This is to the crown and blessing of my life,
The much loved husband of a happy wife;
To him whose constant passion found the art
To win a stubborn and ungrateful heart,
And to the world by tenderest proof discovers
They err, who say that husbands can't be lovers.
With such return of passion, as is due,
Daphnis I love, Daphnis my thoughts pursue;
Daphnis, my hopes and joys are bounded all in you.
Even I, for Daphnis' and my promise' sake,
What I in woman censure, undertake.
But this from love, not vanity proceeds;
You know who writes, and I who 'tis that reads.
Judge not my passion by my want of skill:
Many love well, though they express it ill;
And I your censure could with pleasure bear,
Would you but soon return, and speak it here.

Anne Finch

Longing

Come to me in my dréams, and then
By day I shall be well again!
For then the night will more than pay
The hopeless longing of the day.

Come, as thou cam'st a thousand times,
A messenger from radiant climes,
And smile on thy new world, and be
As kind to others as to me!

Or, as thou never cam'st in sooth,
Come now, and let me dream it truth,
And part my hair, and kiss my brow,
And say, *My love! why sufferest thou?*

Come to me in my dreams, and then
By day I shall be well again!
For then the night will more than pay
The hopeless longing of the day.

Matthew Arnold

Sudden Light

I have been here before,
But when or how I cannot tell:
I know the grass beyond the door,
The sweet keen smell,
The sighing sound, the lights around the shore.

You have been mine before,—
How long ago I may not know:
But just when at that swallow's soar
Your neck turned so,
Some veil did fall,—I knew it all of yore.

Has this been thus before?
And shall not thus time's eddying flight
Still with our lives our love restore
In death's despite,
And day and night yield one delight once more?

Dante Gabriel Rossetti

Love Is Enough

Love is enough: though the World be a-waning,
And the woods have no voice but the voice of
  complaining,
  Though the sky be too dark for dim eyes to discover
The gold-cups and daisies fair blooming thereunder,
Though the hills be held shadows, and the sea a dark
  wonder,
  And this day draw a veil over all deeds pass'd over,
Yet their hands shall not tremble, their feet shall not
  falter;
The void shall not weary, the fear shall not alter
  These lips and these eyes of the loved and the lover.

William Morris

The World Is Too Much with Us

The world is too much with us; late and soon,
Getting and spending, we lay waste our powers;—
Little we see in Nature that is ours;
We have given our hearts away, a sordid boon!
This Sea that bares her bosom to the moon;
The winds that will be howling at all hours,
And are up-gathered now like sleeping flowers;
For this, for everything, we are out of tune;
It moves us not. Great God! I'd rather be
A Pagan suckled in a creed outworn;
So might I, standing on this pleasant lea,
Have glimpses that would make me less forlorn;
Have sight of Proteus rising from the sea;
Or hear old Triton blow his wreathèd horn.

William Wordsworth

Neutral Tones

We stood by a pond that winter day,
And the sun was white, as though chidden of God,
And a few leaves lay on the starving sod;
– They had fallen from an ash, and were gray.

Your eyes on me were as eyes that rove
Over tedious riddles of years ago;
And some words played between us to and fro
On which lost the more by our love.

The smile on your mouth was the deadest thing
Alive enough to have strength to die;
And a grin of bitterness swept thereby
Like an ominous bird a-wing....

Since then, keen lessons that love deceives,
And wrings with wrong, have shaped to me
Your face, and the God curst sun, and a tree,
And a pond edged with grayish leaves.

Thomas Hardy

Tell Me, Dearest, What Is Love?

Tell me, dearest, what is Love?
'Tis a lightning from above,
'Tis an Arrow, 'tis a Fire,
'Tis a boy they call Desire.
  'Tis a Grave
  Gapes to have
Those poor Fools that long to prove.

Tell me more, are Women true?
Yes, some are, and some as you;
Some are willing, some are strange,
Since you men first taught to change.
  And till truth
  Be in both
All shall love to love anew.

Tell me more yet, can they grieve?
Yes, and sicken sore, but live:
And be wise and delay,
When you Men are as wise as they.
  Then I see
  Faith will be
Never till they both believe.

Francis Beaumont

Bequest

You left me, sweet, two legacies,—
A legacy of love
A Heavenly Father would content,
Had He the offer of;

You left me boundaries of pain
Capacious as the sea,
Between eternity and time,
Your consciousness and me.

Emily Dickinson

To Be One With Each Other

What greater thing is there for two human souls
than to feel that they are joined together to strengthen
each other in all labor, to minister to each other in all
   sorrow,
to share with each other in all gladness,
to be one with each other in the
silent unspoken memories?

George Eliot

Because She Would Ask Me Why I Loved Her

If questioning would make us wise
No would ever gaze in;
If all our tale were told in speech
No mouths would wander each to each.
Were spirits free from mortal mesh
And love not bound in hearts of flesh
No aching breasts would yearn to meet
And find their ecstasy complete.
For who is there that lives and knows
The secret powers by which he grows?
Were knowledge all, what were our need
To thrill and faint and sweetly bleed?
Then seek not, sweet, the "If" and "Why"
I love you now until I die.
For I must love because I live
And in me is what you give.

Christopher Brennan

A Valentine To My Wife

Accept, dear girl, this little token,
And if between the lines you seek,
You'll find the love I've often spoken
The love my dying lips shall speak.

Our little ones are making merry
O'er am'rous ditties rhymed in jest,
But in these words (though awkward very)
The genuine article's expressed.

You are as fair and sweet and tender,
Dear brown-eyed little sweetheart mine,
As when, a callow youth and slender,
I asked to be your Valentine.

What though these years of ours be fleeting?
What though the years of youth be flown?
I'll mock old Tempus with repeating,
"I love my love and her alone!"

And when I fall before his reaping,
And when my stuttering speech is dumb,
Think not my love is dead or sleeping,
But that it waits for you to come.

So take, dear love, this little token,
And if there speaks in any line
The sentiment I'd fain have spoken,
Say, will you kiss your Valentine?

Eugene Field

There is a Lady sweet and kind

There is a Lady sweet and kind,
Was never face so pleased my mind;
I did but see her passing by,
And yet I love her till I die.

Her gesture, motion, and her smiles,
Her wit, her voice my heart beguiles,
Beguiles my heart, I know not why,
And yet I love her till I die.

Cupid is wingèd and doth range,
Her country so my love doth change:
But change she earth, or change she sky,
Yet will I love her till I die.

Thomas Ford

To Anthea,
who may Command him Anything

Bid me to live, and I will live
Thy protestant to be;
Or bid me love, and I will give
A loving heart to thee.

A heart as soft, a heart as kind,
A heart as sound and free,
As in the whole world thou canst find,
That heart I'll give to thee.

Bid that heart stay, and it will stay,
To honour thy decree;
Or bid it languish quite away,
And 't shall do so for thee.

Bid me to weep, and I will weep,
While I have eyes to see;
And having none, yet I will keep
A heart to weep for thee.

Bid me despair, and I'll despair,
Under that cypress tree;
Or bid me die, and I will dare
E'en death, to die for thee.

Thou art my life, my love, my heart,
The very eyes of me;
And hast command of every part,
To live and die for thee.

Robert Herrick

In Excelsis

You—you—
Your shadow is sunlight on a plate of silver;
Your footsteps, the seeding-place of lilies;
Your hands moving, a chime of bells across a windless
air.

The movement of your hands is the long, golden
running of light from a rising sun;
It is the hopping of birds upon a garden-path.

As the perfume of jonquils, you come forth in the
morning.
Young horses are not more sudden than your thoughts,
Your words are bees about a pear-tree,
Your fancies are the gold-and-black striped wasps
buzzing among red apples.
I drink your lips,
I eat the whiteness of your hands and feet.
My mouth is open,
As a new jar I am empty and open.
Like white water are you who fill the cup of my mouth,
Like a brook of water thronged with lilies.

You are frozen as the clouds,
You are far and sweet as the high clouds.
I dare to reach to you,
I dare to touch the rim of your brightness.
I leap beyond the winds,
I cry and shout,

For my throat is keen as is a sword
Sharpened on a hone of ivory.
My throat sings the joy of my eyes,
The rushing gladness of my love.

How has the rainbow fallen upon my heart?
How have I snared the seas to lie in my fingers
And caught the sky to be a cover for my head? How
   have you come to dwell with me,
Compassing me with the four circles of your mystic
   lightness,
So that I say "Glory! Glory!" and bow before you
As to a shrine?

Do I tease myself that morning is morning and a day
   after?
Do I think the air is a condescension,
The earth a politeness,
Heaven a boon deserving thanks?
So you—air—earth—heaven—
I do not thank you,
I take you,
I live.
And those things which I say in consequence
Are rubies mortised in a gate of stone.

Amy Lowell

To Amarantha,
That she would dishevell her haire

Amarantha, sweet and fair,
Forbear to braid that shining hair;
As my curious hand or eye,
Hovering round thee, let it fly:
Let it fly as unconfined
As its ravisher the wind,
Who has left his darling east
To wanton o'er this spicy nest.
Every tress must be confess'd
But neatly tangled at the best,
Like a clew of golden thread,
Most excellently ravelled.
Do not then wind up that light
In ribands, and o'ercloud the night;
Like the sun in his early ray,
But shake your head and scatter day.

Richard Lovelace

The Sorrow of True Love

The sorrow of true love is a great sorrow
And true love parting blackens a bright morrow:
Yet almost they equal joys, since their despair
Is but hope blinded by its tears, and clear
Above the storm the heavens wait to be seen.
But greater sorrow from less love has been
That can mistake lack of despair for hope
And knows not tempest and the perfect scope
Of summer, but a frozen drizzle perpetual
Of drops that from remorse and pity fall
And cannot ever shine in the sun or thaw,
Removed eternally from the sun's law.

Edward Thomas

Complaint of a Lover Rebuked

Love, that liveth and reigneth in my thought,
That built his seat within my captive breast,
Clad in the arms wherein with me he fought,
Oft in my face he doth his banner rest:
She that me taught to love and suffer pain,
My doubtful hope and eke my hot desire
With shamefaced cloak to shadow and restrain,
Her smiling grace converteth straight to ire:
And coward Love then to the heart apace
Taketh his flight, whereas he lurks and plains
His purpose lost, and dare not show his face.
For my lord's guilt, thus faultless, bide I pains:
  Yet from my lord shall not my foot remove;
  Sweet is his death that takes his end by Love!

Henry Howard

Extract from Hymen's Triumph

Ah! I remember well (and how can I
But evermore remember well) when first
Our flame began, when scarce we knew what was
The flame we felt; when as we sat and sigh'd
And look'd upon each other, and conceived
Not what we ail'd—yet something we did ail;
And yet were well, and yet we were not well,
And what was our disease we could not tell.
Then would we kiss, then sigh, then look; and thus
In that first garden of our simpleness
We spent our childhood. But when years began
To reap the fruit of knowledge, ah, how then
Would she with graver looks, with sweet, stern brow,
Check my presumption and my forwardness;
Yet still would give me flowers, still would me show
What she would have me, yet not have me know.

Samuel Daniel

I Would Live in Your Love

I would live in your love as the sea-grasses live in the
    sea,
Borne up by each wave as it passes, drawn down by
    each wave that recedes;
I would empty my soul of the dreams that have
    gathered in me,
I would beat with your heart as it beats, I would follow
    your soul as it leads.

Sara Teasdale

Kinds of Love

Foolish love is only folly;
Wanton love is too unholy;
Greedy love is covetous;
Idle love is frivolous;
But the gracious love is it
That doth prove the work of wit.

Beauty but deceives the eye;
Flattery leads the ear awry;
Wealth doth but enchant the wit;
Want, the overthrow of it;
While in Wisdom's worthy grace,
Virtue sees the sweetest face.

There hath Love found out his life,
Peace without all thought of strife;
Kindness in Discretion's care;
Truth, that clearly doth declare
Faith doth in true fancy prove,
Lust the excrements of Love.

Then in faith may fancy see
How my love may construèd be;
How it grows and what it seeks;
How it lives and what it likes;
So in highest grace regard it,
Or in lowest scorn discard it.

Robert Greene

Le Triste Adieu

Oft have we parted Love! before
With prospects darkly shadow'd o'er,
But never have we sunder'd yet,
   With such wild hopelessness as now,
Since first by fate's caprice we met,
Since first upon each heart was set,
   Too powerful love's recorded vow.
Oh! absence were enough to bear
Without the death-spell of despair!
There is no joy on earth to me
   Where thou art not—I sigh to hear
That voice of tend'rest melody
   Still breathe its sweetness to mine ear;
And words from other lips than thine
   Pass, like the winds, unheeded by;
They cannot cheer this breast of mine,
Which ev'n in palaces would pine,
   For thy dear tone's soft witchery.
Smiles, beautiful as thought can paint,
To me would seem but pale and faint
If I must vainly seek the one,
Whose brightness o'er my soul hath shone;
And eyes of richest light, might beam
Like stars upon me, when their gleam,
Hath pour'd upon the midnight sky,
Its fulness of resplendency;
But dim to me would seem their ray,
   If thine were distant:—I should turn
From sunniest looks in grief away,
   O'er our divided lot to mourn.

Thou think'st my heart is colder grown
Amidst the storms we both have known;
No, thou dost wrong me, dearest!—still
Throbs its warm life-pulse but for thee,
With most intense devotion's thrill,
Nor gloomiest hours of gath'ring ill,
    Can shake its deep fidelity.
Wilt thou, with truth as holy, keep
    Affection's glow, unchang'd, and pure?
Shall no dim cloud upon it creep,
    When wealth's gay scenes thy steps allure
In Pleasure's halls, a welcome guest,
Thou wilt be courted, and carest,
And smil'd on by the loveliest!
And wilt thou not too greatly prize
The world's bewildering flatteries,
To dwell, with gentle thoughts, on one,
Whose best, and happiest days, are gone;
And o'er whose path-way tempests throw
    The threat'nings of their angry wing,
Whose ambush'd thunder, soon below
    May burst, in bolts of suffering.
Thy web of destiny was wrought,
In colours from the rainbow caught;
And golden threads were blended there,
With silken lines of promise fair,
Mine, was the woof of sadden'd grey,
    Unmix'd with aught of brilliant hue;
Fram'd in its varyings to display
    No tints, but those to sorrow true.
And thou perhaps would'st break the chain,
    Entwin'd around us, ere we knew

How heavily its weight of pain,
  Would oft thy mind's repose subdue:—
Let not the cares which round me cling,
  Obscure one moment's bliss for thee;—
But sever fearlessly the string—
The lingering cord—which will but bring
  Grief!—if it link thee still to me !
Go!—shine where tears are never shed,
  And leave me to my lonely doom:
Soon will my love with life be fled,
  And rest will greet me,—in the tomb!

Eliza Acton

Happiness

This perfect love can find no words to say.
What words are left, still sacred for our use,
That have not suffered the sad world's abuse,
And figure forth a gladness dimmed and gray?
Let us be silent still, since words convey
But shadowed images, wherein we lose
The fulness of love's light; our lips refuse
The fluent commonplace of yesterday.
Then shall we hear beneath the brooding wing
Of silence what abiding voices sleep,
The primal notes of nature, that outring
Man's little noises, warble he or weep,
The song the morning stars together sing,
The sound of deep that calleth unto deep.

Edith Wharton

At Last

At last, when all the summer shine
That warmed life's early hours is past,
Your loving fingers seek for mine
And hold them close—at last—at last!
Not oft the robin comes to build
Its nest upon the leafless bough
By autumn robbed, by winter chilled,—
But you, dear heart, you love me now.

Though there are shadows on my brow
And furrows on my cheek, in truth,—
The marks where Time's remorseless plough
Broke up the blooming sward of Youth,—
Though fled is every girlish grace
Might win or hold a lover's vow,
Despite my sad and faded face,
And darkened heart, you love me now!

I count no more my wasted tears;
They left no echo of their fall;
I mourn no more my lonesome years;
This blessed hour atones for all.
I fear not all that Time or Fate
May bring to burden heart or brow,—
Strong in the love that came so late,
Our souls shall keep it always now!

Elizabeth Akers Allen

The Passionate Shepherd to His Love

Come live with me and be my love,
And we will all the pleasures prove,
That Valleys, groves, hills, and fields,
Woods, or steepy mountain yields.

And we will sit upon the Rocks,
Seeing the Shepherds feed their flocks,
By shallow Rivers to whose falls
Melodious birds sing Madrigals.

And I will make thee beds of Roses
And a thousand fragrant posies,
A cap of flowers, and a kirtle
Embroidered all with leaves of Myrtle;

A gown made of the finest wool
Which from our pretty Lambs we pull;
Fair lined slippers for the cold,
With buckles of the purest gold;

A belt of straw and Ivy buds,
With Coral clasps and Amber studs:
And if these pleasures may thee move,
Come live with me, and be my love.

The Shepherds' Swains shall dance and sing
For thy delight each May-morning:
If these delights thy mind may move,
Then live with me, and be my love.

Christopher Marlowe

When I Was One-and-Twenty

When I was one-and-twenty
    I heard a wise man say,
"Give crowns and pounds and guineas
    But not your heart away;
Give pearls away and rubies
    But keep your fancy free."
But I was one-and-twenty,
    No use to talk to me.

When I was one-and-twenty
    I heard him say again,
"The heart out of the bosom
    Was never given in vain;
'Tis paid with sighs a plenty
    And sold for endless rue."
And I am two-and-twenty,
    And oh, 'tis true, 'tis true.

A. E. Housman

Requiescat

Strew on her roses, roses,
And never a spray of yew!
In quiet she reposes;
Ah, would that I did too!

Her mirth the world required;
She bathed it in smiles of glee.
But her heart was tired, tired,
And now they let her be.

Her life was turning, turning,
In mazes of heat and sound.
But for peace her soul was yearning,
And now peace laps her round.

Her cabin'd, ample spirit,
It flutter'd and fail'd for breath.
To-night it doth inherit
The vasty hall of death.

Matthew Arnold

When My Love Did What I Would Not

When my love did what I would not, what I would not,
I could hear his merry voice upon the wind,
Crying, "Fairest, shut your eyes, for see you should not.
Love is blind!"

When my love said what I say not, what I say not,
With a joyous laugh he quieted my fears,
Whispering, "Fairest, hearken not, for hear you may
  not.
Hath Love ears?"

When my love said, "Will you longer let me seek it?
Blind and deaf is she that doth not bid me come!"
All my heart said murmuring, "Dearest, can I speak it?
Love is dumb."

Mary Elizabeth Coleridge

The Married Lover

Why, having won her, do I woo?
Because her spirit's vestal grace
Provokes me always to pursue,
But, spirit-like, eludes embrace;
Because her womanhood is such
That, as on court-days subjects kiss
The Queen's hand, yet so near a touch
Affirms no mean familiarness,
Nay, rather marks more fair the height
Which can with safety so neglect
To dread, as lower ladies might,
That grace could meet with disrespect;
Thus she with happy favor feeds
Allegiance from a love so high
That thence no false conceit proceeds
Of difference bridged, or state put by;
Because, although in act and word
As lowly as a wife can be
Her manners, when they call me lord,
Remind me 'tis by courtesy;
Not with her least consent of will,
Which would my proud affection hurt,
But by the noble style that still
Imputes an unattained desert;
Because her gay and lofty brows,
When all is won which hope can ask,
Reflect a light of hopeless snows
That bright in virgin ether bask;

Because, though free of the outer court
I am, this Temple keeps its shrine
Sacred to heaven; because, in short,
She's not and never can be mine.

Coventry Patmore

Her Voice

The wild bee reels from bough to bough
With his furry coat and his gauzy wing,
Now in a lily-cup, and now
Setting a jacinth bell a-swing,
In his wandering;
Sit closer love: it was here I trow
I made that vow,

Swore that two lives should be like one
As long as the sea-gull loved the sea,
As long as the sunflower sought the sun,—
It shall be, I said, for eternity
'Twixt you and me!
Dear friend, those times are over and done;
Love's web is spun.

Look upward where the poplar trees
Sway and sway in the summer air,
Here in the valley never a breeze
Scatters the thistledown, but there
Great winds blow fair
From the mighty murmuring mystical seas,
And the wave-lashed leas.

Look upward where the white gull screams,
What does it see that we do not see?
Is that a star? or the lamp that gleams
On some outward voyaging argosy,

Ah! can it be
We have lived our lives in a land of dreams!
How sad it seems.

Sweet, there is nothing left to say
But this, that love is never lost,
Keen winter stabs the breasts of May
Whose crimson roses burst his frost,
Ships tempest-tossed
Will find a harbour in some bay,
And so we may.

And there is nothing left to do
But to kiss once again, and part,
Nay, there is nothing we should rue,
I have my beauty,—you your Art,
Nay, do not start,
One world was not enough for two
Like me and you.

Oscar Wilde

Fidelity

Man and woman are like the earth, that brings forth
　　flowers in summer, and love, but underneath is rock.

Older than flowers, older than ferns, older than
　　foraminiferae older than plasm altogether is the soul
　　underneath.

And when, throughout all the wild chaos of love
slowly a gem forms, in the ancient, once-more-molten
　　rocks
of two human hearts, two ancient rocks
a man's heart and a woman's
that is the crystal of peace, the slow hard jewel of trust,
the sapphire of fidelity.

The gem of mutual peace emerging from the wild
　　chaos of love.

D. H. Lawrence

On the Balcony

In front of the sombre mountains, a faint, lost ribbon of
   rainbow;
And between us and it, the thunder;
And down below in the green wheat, the labourers
Stand like dark stumps, still in the green wheat.

You are near to me, and your naked feet in their
   sandals,
And through the scent of the balcony's naked timber
I distinguish the scent of your hair: so now the limber
Lightning falls from heaven.

Adown the pale-green glacier river floats
A dark boat through the gloom—and whither?
The thunder roars. But still we have each other!
The naked lightnings in the heavens dither
And disappear—what have we but each other?
The boat has gone.

D. H. Lawrence

When You Are Old

When you are old and grey and full of sleep,
And nodding by the fire, take down this book,
And slowly read, and dream of the soft look
Your eyes had once, and of their shadows deep;

How many loved your moments of glad grace,
And loved your beauty with love false or true,
But one man loved the pilgrim soul in you,
And loved the sorrows of your changing face;

And bending down beside the glowing bars,
Murmur, a little sadly, how Love fled
And paced upon the mountains overhead
And hid his face amid a crowd of stars.

W. B. Yeats

Love (III)

Love bade me welcome. Yet my soul drew back
　　Guilty of dust and sin.
But quick-eyed Love, observing me grow slack
　　From my first entrance in,
Drew nearer to me, sweetly questioning,
　　If I lacked any thing.

A guest, I answered, worthy to be here:
　　Love said, You shall be he.
I the unkind, ungrateful? Ah my dear,
　　I cannot look on thee.
Love took my hand, and smiling did reply,
　　Who made the eyes but I?

Truth Lord, but I have marred them: let my shame
　　Go where it doth deserve.
And know you not, says Love, who bore the blame?
　　My dear, then I will serve.
You must sit down, says Love, and taste my meat:
　　So I did sit and eat.

George Herbert

Love in the Valley

Under yonder beech-tree single on the green-sward,
Couched with her arms behind her golden head,
Knees and tresses folded to slip and ripple idly,
Lies my young love sleeping in the shade.
Had I the heart to slide an arm beneath her,
Press her parting lips as her waist I gather slow,
Waking in amazement she could not but embrace me:
Then would she hold me and never let me go?

Shy as the squirrel and wayward as the swallow,
Swift as the swallow along the river's light
Circleting the surface to meet his mirrored winglets,
Fleeter she seems in her stay than in her flight.
Shy as the squirrel that leaps among the pine-tops,
Wayward as the swallow overhead at set of sun,
She whom I love is hard to catch and conquer,
Hard, but O the glory of the winning were she won!

When her mother tends her before the laughing mirror,
Tying up her laces, looping up her hair,
Often she thinks, were this wild thing wedded,
More love should I have, and much less care.
When her mother tends her before the lighted mirror,
Loosening her laces, combing down her curls,
Often she thinks, were this wild thing wedded,
I should miss but one for many boys and girls.

Heartless she is as the shadow in the meadows
Flying to the hills on a blue and breezy noon.
No, she is athirst and drinking up her wonder:

Earth to her is young as the slip of the new moon.
Deals she an unkindness, 'tis but her rapid measure,
Even as in a dance; and her smile can heal no less:
Like the swinging May-cloud that pelts the flowers with
  hailstones
Off a sunny border, she was made to bruise and bless.

Lovely are the curves of the white owl sweeping
Wavy in the dusk lit by one large star.
Lone on the fir-branch, his rattle-note unvaried,
Brooding o'er the gloom, spins the brown eve-jar.
Darker grows the valley, more and more forgetting:
So were it with me if forgetting could be willed.
Tell the grassy hollow that holds the bubbling well-
  spring,
Tell it to forget the source that keeps it filled.

Stepping down the hill with her fair companions,
Arm in arm, all against the raying West
Boldly she sings, to the merry tune she marches,
Brave in her shape, and sweeter unpossessed.
Sweeter, for she is what my heart first awaking
Whispered the world was; morning light is she.
Love that so desires would fain keep her changeless;
Fain would fling the net, and fain have her free.

Happy happy time, when the white star hovers
Low over dim fields fresh with bloomy dew,
Near the face of dawn, that draws athwart the darkness,
Threading it with colour, as yewberries the yew.
Thicker crowd the shades while the grave East deepens
Glowing, and with crimson a long cloud swells.

Maiden still the morn is; and strange she is, and secret;
Strange her eyes; her cheeks are cold as cold sea-shells.

Sunrays, leaning on our southern hills and lighting
Wild cloud-mountains that drag the hills along,
Oft ends the day of your shifting brilliant laughter
Chill as a dull face frowning on a song.
Ay, but shows the South-West a ripple-feathered bosom
Blown to silver while the clouds are shaken and ascend
Scaling the mid-heavens as they stream, there comes a
    sunset
Rich, deep like love in beauty without end.

When at dawn she sighs, and like an infant to the
    window
Turns grave eyes craving light, released from dreams,
Beautiful she looks, like a white water-lily
Bursting out of bud in havens of the streams.
When from bed she rises clothed from neck to ankle
In her long nightgown sweet as boughs of May,
Beautiful she looks, like a tall garden lily
Pure from the night, and splendid for the day.

Mother of the dews, dark eye-lashed twilight,
Low-lidded twilight, o'er the valley's brim,
Rounding on thy breast sings the dew-delighted skylark,
Clear as though the dewdrops had their voice in him.
Hidden where the rose-flush drinks the rayless planet,
Fountain-full he pours the spraying fountain-showers.
Let me hear her laughter, I would have her ever
Cool as dew in twilight, the lark above the flowers.

All the girls are out with their baskets for the primrose;
Up lanes, woods through, they troop in joyful bands.
My sweet leads: she knows not why, but now she
   totters,
Eyes the bent anemones, and hangs her hands.
Such a look will tell that the violets are peeping,
Coming the rose: and unaware a cry
Springs in her bosom for odours and for colour,
Covert and the nightingale; she knows not why.

Kerchiefed head and chin she darts between her tulips,
Streaming like a willow grey in arrowy rain:
Some bend beaten cheek to gravel, and their angel
She will be; she lifts them, and on she speeds again.
Black the driving raincloud breasts the iron gateway:
She is forth to cheer a neighbour lacking mirth.
So when sky and grass met rolling dumb for thunder
Saw I once a white dove, sole light of earth.

Prim little scholars are the flowers of her garden,
Trained to stand in rows, and asking if they please.
I might love them well but for loving more the wild
   ones:
O my wild ones! they tell me more than these.
You, my wild one, you tell of honied field-rose,
Violet, blushing eglantine in life; and even as they,
They by the wayside are earnest of your goodness,
You are of life's, on the banks that line the way.

Peering at her chamber the white crowns the red rose,
Jasmine winds the porch with stars two and three.
Parted is the window; she sleeps; the starry jasmine

Breathes a falling breath that carries thoughts of me.
Sweeter unpossessed, have I said of her my sweetest?
Not while she sleeps: while she sleeps the jasmine
   breathes,
Luring her to love; she sleeps; the starry jasmine
Bears me to her pillow under white rose-wreaths.

Yellow with birdfoot-trefoil are the grass-glades;
Yellow with cinquefoil of the dew-grey leaf;
Yellow with stonecrop; the moss-mounds are yellow;
Blue-necked the wheat sways, yellowing to the sheaf:
Green-yellow bursts from the copse the laughing yaffle;
Sharp as a sickle is the edge of shade and shine:
Earth in her heart laughs looking at the heavens,
Thinking of the harvest: I look and think of mine.

This I may know: her dressing and undressing
Such a change of light shows as when the skies in sport
Shift from cloud to moonlight; or edging over thunder
Slips a ray of sun; or sweeping into port
White sails furl; or on the ocean borders
White sails lean along the waves leaping green.
Visions of her shower before me, but from eyesight
Guarded she would be like the sun were she seen.

Front door and back of the mossed old farmhouse
Open with the morn, and in a breezy link
Freshly sparkles garden to stripe-shadowed orchard,
Green across a rill where on sand the minnows wink.
Busy in the grass the early sun of summer
Swarms, and the blackbird's mellow fluting notes
Call my darling up with round and roguish challenge:

Quaintest, richest carol of all the singing throats!

Cool was the woodside; cool as her white dairy
Keeping sweet the cream-pan; and there the boys from
  school,
Cricketing below, rushed brown and red with sunshine;
O the dark translucence of the deep-eyed cool!
Spying from the farm, herself she fetched a pitcher
Full of milk, and tilted for each in turn the beak.
Then a little fellow, mouth up and on tiptoe,
Said, "I will kiss you": she laughed and leaned her
  cheek.

Doves of the fir-wood walling high our red roof
Through the long noon coo, crooning through the coo.
Loose droop the leaves, and down the sleepy roadway
Sometimes pipes a chaffinch; loose droops the blue.
Cows flap a slow tail knee-deep in the river,
Breathless, given up to sun and gnat and fly.
Nowhere is she seen; and if I see her nowhere,
Lightning may come, straight rains and tiger sky.

O the golden sheaf, the rustling treasure-armful!
O the nutbrown tresses nodding interlaced!
O the treasure-tresses one another over
Nodding! O the girdle slack about the waist!
Slain are the poppies that shot their random scarlet
Quick amid the wheatears: wound about the waist,
Gathered, see these brides of Earth one blush of
  ripeness!
O the nutbrown tresses nodding interlaced!

Large and smoky red the sun's cold disk drops,
Clipped by naked hills, on violet shaded snow:
Eastward large and still lights up a bower of moonrise,
Whence at her leisure steps the moon aglow.
Nightlong on black print-branches our beech-tree
Gazes in this whiteness: nightlong could I.
Here may life on death or death on life be painted.
Let me clasp her soul to know she cannot die!

Gossips count her faults; they scour a narrow chamber
Where there is no window, read not heaven or her.
"When she was a tiny," one aged woman quavers,
Plucks at my heart and leads me by the ear.
Faults she had once as she learnt to run and tumbled:
Faults of feature some see, beauty not complete.
Yet, good gossips, beauty that makes holy
Earth and air, may have faults from head to feet.

Hither she comes; she comes to me; she lingers,
Deepens her brown eyebrows, while in new surprise
High rise the lashes in wonder of a stranger;
Yet am I the light and living of her eyes.
Something friends have told her fills her heart to
  brimming,
Nets her in her blushes, and wounds her, and tames—
Sure of her haven, O like a dove alighting,
Arms up, she dropped: our souls were in our names.

Soon will she lie like a white-frost sunrise.
Yellow oats and brown wheat, barley pale as rye,
Long since your sheaves have yielded to the thresher,
Felt the girdle loosened, seen the tresses fly.

Soon will she lie like a blood-red sunset.
Swift with the to-morrow, green-winged Spring!
Sing from the South-West, bring her back the truants,
Nightingale and swallow, song and dipping wing.

Soft new beech-leaves, up to beamy April
Spreading bough on bough a primrose mountain, you,
Lucid in the moon, raise lilies to the skyfields,
Youngest green transfused in silver shining through:
Fairer than the lily, than the wild white cherry:
Fair as in image my seraph love appears
Borne to me by dreams when dawn is at my eyelids:
Fair as in the flesh she swims to me on tears.

Could I find a place to be alone with heaven,
I would speak my heart out: heaven is my need.
Every woodland tree is flushing like the dog-wood,
Flashing like the whitebeam, swaying like the reed.
Flushing like the dog-wood crimson in October;
Streaming like the flag-reed South-West blown;
Flashing as in gusts the sudden-lighted white beam:
All seem to know what is for heaven alone.

George Meredith

Farewell to Matilda

Oui, pour jamais
  Chassons l'image
  De la volage
    Que j'adorais.   PARNY.

Matilda, farewell! Fate has doom'd us to part,
But the prospect occasions no pang to my heart;
No longer is love with my reason at strife,
Though once thou wert dearer, far dearer than life.

As together we roam'd, I the passion confess'd,
Which thy beauty and virtue had rais'd in my breast;
That the passion was mutual thou mad'st me believe,
And I thought my Matilda could never deceive.

My Matilda! no, false one! my claims I resign:
Thou canst not, thou must not, thou shalt not be mine:
I now scorn thee as much as I lov'd thee before,
Nor sigh when I think I shall meet thee no more.

Though fair be thy form, thou no lovers wilt find,
While folly and falsehood inhabit thy mind,
Though coxcombs may flatter, though ideots may prize,
Thou art shunn'd by the good, and contemn'd by the
  wise.

Than mine what affection more fervent could be,
When I thought ev'ry virtue was center'd in thee?
Of the vows thou hast broken I will not complain,
For I mourn not the loss of a heart I disdain.

Oh! hadst thou but constant and amiable prov'd
As that *fancied perfection* I formerly lov'd,
Nor absence, nor time, though supreme their controul,
Could have dimm'd the dear image then stamp'd on my
  soul.

How bright were the pictures, untinted with shade,
By Hope's glowing pencil on Fancy pourtray'd!
Sweet visions of bliss! which I could not retain;
For they, like thyself, were deceitful and vain.

Some other, perhaps, to Matilda is dear,
Some other, more pleasing, though not more sincere;
May he fix thy light passions, now wav'ring as air,
Then leave thee, inconstant, to shame and despair!

Repent not, Matilda, return not to me:
Unavailing thy grief, thy repentance will be:
In vain will thy vows or thy smiles be resum'd,
For love, once extinguish'd, is never relum'd.

Thomas Love Peacock

A White Rose

The red rose whispers of passion,
And the white rose breathes of love;
O, the red rose is a falcon,
And the white rose is a dove.
But I send you a cream-white rosebud
With a flush on its petal tips;
For the love that is purest and sweetest
Has a kiss of desire on the lips

John Boyle O'Reilly

The White Heliotrope

The feverish room and that white bed,
The tumbled skirts upon a chair,
The novel flung half-open where
Hat, hair-pins, puffs, and paints, are spread;

The mirror that has sucked your face
Into it's secret deep of deeps,
And there mysteriously keeps
Forgotten memories of grace;

And you, half-dressed and half awake,
Your slant eyes strangely watching me,
And I, who watch you drowsily,
With eyes that, having slept not, ache;

This (need one dread? nay, dare one hope?)
Will rise, a ghost of memory, if
Ever again my handkerchief
Is scented with White Heliotrope.

Arthur Symons

Eros

The sense of the world is short,—
Long and various the report,—
　To love and be beloved;
Men and gods have not outlearned it;
And, how oft soe'er they've turned it,
　'Tis not to be improved.

Ralph Waldo Emerson

Maidens II

Maidens the poets learn from you to tell
How solitary and remote you are,
As night is lighted by one high bright star
They draw light from the distance where you dwell.

For poet you must always maiden be
Even though his eyes the woman in you wake
Wedding brocade your fragile wrists would break,
Mysterious, elusive, from him flee.

Within his garden let him wait alone
Where benches stand expectant in the shade
Within the chamber where the lyre was played
Where he received you as the eternal One.

Go! It grows dark—your voice and form no more
His senses seek; he now no longer sees
A white robe fluttering under dark beech trees
Along the pathway where it gleamed before.

He loves the long paths where no footfalls ring,
And he loves much the silent chamber where
Like a soft whisper through the quiet air
He hears your voice, far distant, vanishing.
The softly stealing echo comes again
From crowds of men whom, wearily, he shuns;
And many see you there—so his thought runs—
And tenderest memories are pierced with pain.

Rainer Maria Rilke (tr. Jessie Lemont)

To a Lady

Sweet rois[1] of vertew and of gentilness,
Delytsum lily of everie lustynes,
Richest in bontie and in bewtie clear,
And everie vertew that is wenit[2] dear,
Except onlie that ye are mercyless.

Into your garth[3] this day I did persew,
There saw I flowris that fresche were of hew;
Baith quhyte[4] and reid most lusty were to seynn[5],
And halesome herbis upon stalkis green;
Yet leaf nor flowr find could I nane of rew.

I doubt that Merche, with his cauld blastis keyne,
Has slain this gentle herb, that I of mene;
Quhois[6] piteous death dois to my heart sic paine
That I would make to plant his root againe,—
So confort and his levis unto me bene.

William Dunbar

---

1 rose
2 esteemed
3 garden
4 white
5 see
6 whose

Love and Friendship

Love is like the wild rose-briar,
Friendship like the holly-tree—
The holly is dark when the rose-briar blooms
But which will bloom most constantly?

The wild rose-briar is sweet in spring,
Its summer blossoms scent the air;
Yet wait till winter comes again
And who will call the wild-briar fair?

Then scorn the silly rose-wreath now
And deck thee with the holly's sheen,
That when December blights thy brow
He still may leave thy garland green.

Emily Brontë

The White Birds

I would that we were, my beloved, white birds on the
  foam of the sea!
We tire of the flame of the meteor, before it can fade
  and flee;
And the flame of the blue star of twilight, hung low on
  the rim of the sky,
Has awakened in our hearts, my beloved, a sadness that
  may not die.
A weariness comes from those dreamers, dew-dabbled,
  the lily and rose;
Ah, dream not of them, my beloved, the flame of the
  meteor that goes,
Or the flame of the blue star that lingers hung low in
  the fall of the dew:
For I would we were changed to white birds on the
  wandering foam: I and you!

I am haunted by numberless islands, and many a
  Danaan shore,
Where Time would surely forget us, and Sorrow come
  near us no more;
Soon far from the rose and the lily, and fret of the
  flames would we be,
Were we only white birds, my beloved, buoyed out on
  the foam of the sea!

W. B. Yeats

I Love You

I love your lips when they're wet with wine
And red with a wild desire;
I love your eyes when the lovelight lies
Lit with a passionate fire.
I love your arms when the warm white flesh
Touches mine in a fond embrace;
I love your hair when the strands enmesh
Your kisses against my face.

Not for me the cold, calm kiss
Of a virgin's bloodless love;
Not for me the saint's white bliss,
Nor the heart of a spotless dove.
But give me the love that so freely gives
And laughs at the whole world's blame,
With your body so young and warm in my arms,
It sets my poor heart aflame.

So kiss me sweet with your warm wet mouth,
Still fragrant with ruby wine,
And say with a fervor born of the South
That your body and soul are mine.
Clasp me close in your warm young arms,
While the pale stars shine above,
And we'll live our whole young lives away
In the joys of a living love.

Ella Wheeler Wilcox

The Nymph's Reply to the Shepherd

If all the world and Love were young,
And truth in every shepherd's tongue,
These pretty pleasures might me move
To live with thee and be thy love.
But time drives flocks from field to fold,
When rivers rage, and rocks grow cold;
Then Philomel becometh dumb,
The rest complains of cares to come.
The flowers do fade, and wanton fields
To wayward winter reckoning yields;
A honey tongue, a heart of gall,
Is fancy's spring: but sorrow's fall.
Thy gowns, thy shoes, thy bed of roses,
Thy cup, thy kirtle, and thy posies,
Soon break, soon wither, soon forgotten;—
In folly ripe, in reason rotten.
The belt of straw and ivy-buds,
Thy coral clasps and amber studs,—
All these in me no means can move,
To come to thee, and be thy love.
What should we talk of dainties, then,
Of better meat than's fit for men?
These are but vain: that's only good
Which God hath bless'd and sent for food.

But could youth last, and love still breed;
Had joys no date, nor age no need;
Then those delights my mind might move,
To live with thee, and be thy love.

Sir Walter Raleigh

My Dear and Only Love

My dear and only Love, I pray
   This noble world of thee
Be govern'd by no other sway
   But purest monarchy;
For if confusion have a part,
   Which virtuous souls abhor,
And hold a synod in thy heart,
   I'll never love thee more.

Like Alexander I will reign,
   And I will reign alone,
My thoughts shall evermore disdain
   A rival on my throne.
He either fears his fate too much,
   Or his deserts are small,
That puts it not unto the touch
   To win or lose it all.

But I must rule and govern still,
   And always give the law,
And have each subject at my will,
   And all to stand in awe.
But 'gainst my battery, if I find
   Thou shunn'st the prize so sore
As that thou sett'st me up a blind,
   I'll never love thee more.

Or in the empire of thy heart,
  Where I should solely be,
Another do pretend a part
  And dares to vie with me;
Or if committees thou erect,
  And go on such a score,
I'll sing and laugh at thy neglect,
  And never love thee more.

But if thou wilt be constant then,
  And faithful of thy word,
I'll make thee glorious by my pen
  And famous by my sword:
I'll serve thee in such noble ways
  Was never heard before;
I'll crown and deck thee all with bays,
  And love thee evermore.

James Graham, Marquis of Montrose

My Dearest Dust

My dearest dust, could not thy hasty day
Afford thy drowzy patience leave to stay
One hower longer: so that we might either
Sate up, or gone to bedd together?
But since thy finisht labor hath possest
Thy weary limbs with early rest,
Enjoy it sweetly: and thy widdowe bride
Shall soone repose her by thy slumbring side.
Whose business, now, is only to prepare
My nightly dress, and call to prayre:
Mine eyes wax heavy and ye day growes old.
The dew falls thick, my beloved growes cold.
Draw, draw ye closed curtaynes: and make room:
My dear, my dearest dust; I come, I come.

Lady Katherine Dyer

I Have Loved Flowers That Fade

I have lov'd flowers that fade,
Within whose magic tents
Rich hues have marriage made
With sweet unmemoried scents:
A honeymoon delight,—
A joy of love at sight,
That ages in an hour:—
My song be like a flower!

I have lov'd airs that die
Before their charm is writ
Along a liquid sky
Trembling to welcome it.
Notes, that with pulse of fire
Proclaim the spirit's desire,
Then die, and are nowhere:—
My song be like an air!

Die, song, die like a breath,
And wither as a bloom:
Fear not a flowery death,
Dread not an airy tomb!
Fly with delight, fly hence!
'T was thine love's tender sense
To feast; now on thy bier
Beauty shall shed a tear.

Robert Bridges

Love's Land

Oh! Love builds on the azure sea,
And Love builds on the golden strand,
And Love builds on the rose-winged cloud,
And sometimes Love builds on the land.

Oh! if Love build on sparkling sea,
And if Love build on golden strand,
And if Love build on rosy cloud,
To Love these are the solid land.

Oh! Love will build his lily walls,
And Love his pearly roof will rear
On cloud, or land, or mist, or sea—
Love's solid land is everywhere!

Isabella Crawford

Sylvia

The Nymph that undoes me, is fair and unkind;
No less than a wonder by Nature designed.
She's the grief of my heart, the joy of my eye;
And the cause of a flame that never can die!

Her mouth, from whence wit still obligingly flows,
Has the beautiful blush, and the smell, of the rose.
Love and Destiny both attend on her will;
She wounds with a look; with a frown, she can kill!

The desperate Lover can hope no redress;
Where Beauty and Rigour are both in excess!
In Sylvia they meet; so unhappy am I!
Who sees her, must love; and who loves her, must die!

Sir George Etherege

Believe Me, If All Those Endearing Young Charms

Believe me, if all those endearing young charms,
Which I gaze on so fondly to-day,
Were to change by to-morrow, and fleet in my arms,
Like fairy-gifts, fading away!
Thou wouldst still be ador'd as this moment thou art,
Let thy loveliness fade as it will;
And, around the dear ruin, each wish of my heart
Would entwine itself verdantly still!

It is not while beauty and youth are thine own,
And thy cheeks unprofan'd by a tear,
That the fervour and faith of a soul can be known,
To which time will but make thee more dear!
Oh! the heart, that has truly lov'd, never forgets,
But as truly loves on to the close;
As the sun-flower turns on her god, when he sets,
The same look which she turn'd when he rose!

Thomas Moore

The Meeting

We started speaking,
Looked at each other, then turned away.
The tears kept rising to my eyes
But I could not weep.
I wanted to take your hand
But my hand trembled.
You kept counting the days
Before we should meet again.
But both of us felt in our hearts
That we parted for ever and ever.
The ticking of the little clock filled the quiet room.
"Listen," I said. "It is so loud,
Like a horse galloping on a lonely road,
As loud as that-a horse galloping past in the night."
You shut me up in your arms.

But the sound of the clock stifled our hearts' beating.
You said, "I cannot go: all that is living of me
Is here for ever and ever."
Then you went.

The world changed. The sound of the clock grew
    fainter,
Dwindled away, became a minute thing.
I whispered in the darkness, "If it stops, I shall die."

Katherine Mansfield

Index of First Lines